HOW TO
TRAIN YOURSELF TO SUCCEED
IN SELLING

HOW TO TRAIN YOURSELF TO
SUCCEED
IN SELLING

Alfred Tack

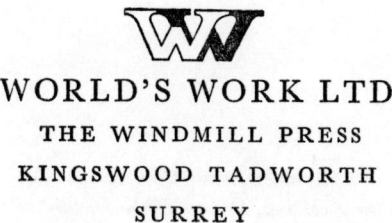

WORLD'S WORK LTD
THE WINDMILL PRESS
KINGSWOOD TADWORTH
SURREY

Made and printed in Great Britain by
William Clowes and Sons, Limited, London, Beccles and Colchester

For
the best of all publishers
my very good friend
Phyllis Alexander

CONTENTS

CHAPTER I

THE CHANGE IN SALESMANSHIP

What are the major changes in selling over the last thirty years? Is the salesman of today inferior to his counterpart of the '30's?

There have been practically no changes in the techniques of selling for many, many years, and the salesmen of the '60's are superior to their predecessors selling between the wars. However it is an accepted belief that men selling between 1928 and 1939 were ambitious, determined, enthusiastic, and highly skilled in the art of salesmanship. But here is an extract from an article on salesmen printed in the *Star*, the former London evening newspaper, before the war:

Why isn't management doing something about training salesmen? The present-day representative is far inferior to the old-time commercial traveller. Before the 1914-1918 war men on the road took pride in their appearance and understood the needs of their customers. They were not high pressure men, but they knew their products and were guided by a sense of purpose. By comparison, the salesman today lacks moral fibre, and sometimes barely understands what common courtesy means . . .

Isn't that the kind of criticism of salesmen that we hear today? Nothing, after all, seems to change very much. Too many people weave dreams of what they thought happened in the past. The dynamic sales director asserts that, when he was a salesman, men did *this* and men did *that*. They probably didn't do either *this* or *that*, but myths of the past die hard. Here is another pre-war extract from the *Efficiency Magazine*:

Will salesmen become redundant? More and more stores are cen-

tralising their buying. Others are setting up special buying depart-ments, and representatives are asked to leave their goods with the commissionaire and return later for the verdict of the committee of buyers. How can true salesmanship—the ability to help a customer arrive at a correct decision—be practised if the buyers are not seen?

And what happens today? The modern salesman, especial-ly in the consumer field, blames the buying committees of self-service stores, grocery chains, and multiple stores, for his lack of success.

High pressure selling

Because of unemployment from 1920–1930, many men gravitated towards salesmanship, which, in those days, so often meant remuneration by commission only. It was the only work they could get. This, as a consequence, led to what is loosely called high pressure selling.

What is high pressure selling? Is it a determination to suc-ceed, forcefulness which brings results, dedicated enthusiasm? None of these. Every good salesman should be determined, forceful, and enthusiastic. High pressure selling is fraudulent selling. It's as simple as that.

It may be true that the hungry fighter fights better, but the hungry salesman more often than not misrepresents. When a fast-talking door-to-door salesman bewilders some poor house-wife with his half-truths and exaggerations, he is a crook. When a salesman misleads a prospect, he is a crook. When a salesman keeps his hand over the small print on an order form, thus concealing from the prospect that he is placing a firm order and not obtaining goods on sale or return, he is a crook. When a salesman indulges in switch selling, knowing full well that he will never sell the cheaper advertised model, he is a crook. When a salesman selling books pretends he has been sent by the local education committee, he is a crook. That is high pressure selling. It has not changed over thirty years, because crooks don't change.

Be aggressive!

You may have heard that salesmen were more aggressive years ago and there is a great need now for aggressive salesmen. What does an aggressive salesman do? Here is a dictionary definition of the word 'aggressive':

> *begin a quarrel; to intrude; first act of hostility or injury; making the first attack or prone to do so; offensive as opposed to defensive.*

Does this help us? Do we want salesmen to *'begin a quarrel'* or to *'make the first attack'*? Maybe there is something in being *'offensive'* rather than *'defensive'*, but if we check on the word *'offensiveness'* we find that it means *'making the first attack'*.

But surely we don't *'attack'* prospective customers. There are a few overbearing salesmen who are supposed to have succeeded because of their pugnacity, but, of course, the real reason for their success is a combination of many other qualities.

Usually, the word 'aggressive' is bandied about by people with little idea of what salesmanship means. Politicians have expressed the view that we need more aggressive selling abroad. Don't they realise that the so-called aggressive salesman has about as much chance of succeeding these days as a British Prime Minister trying similar pugnacity on the President of the U.S.A.? Yet both the salesman and the politician have a similar objective—to influence the mind of another person.

The ordinary person may be misled by the salesmen they see portrayed in films or on television. They are shown either as down-at-heel layabouts, or dynamic go-getters who can thump tables and push their customers around. Both images are very wide of the mark. There was no 'aggressive' selling in the '30's, and I have not met an aggressive salesman during the past twenty years or more, so no one need be ambitious to train himself as heavyweight champion of his sales force.

What about a sales sequence?

Some newcomers might believe that planned selling—in other words, mastering a sales sequence and repeating it at every call—is a recent innovation.

But is it new? John H. Patterson, founder of the National Cash Register Company, originated a sales sequence technique over fifty years ago. It was taught to men in his company for many years. Subsequently, his idea was copied by other companies and used extensively between 1920 and 1936; it is still being used by some organisations today.

The modern version of the planned selling technique originated by the N.C.R. is called the *Selling Sentence* presentation. This has proved very effective, and is now used by salesmen all over the world.

But is it so modern? We originated it in 1935, and have been teaching it ever since.

Pictorial selling

Recently we were approached by an American company and invited to distribute for them in this country their revolutionary plan to make selling easy. They called it *visual aid selling*.

Is this a great advance in salesmanship? The basic idea behind visual aid selling is that, although a salesman should learn a standard sales presentation, he will not always keep to it. The new recruit to selling may, through sheer nervousness, forget a part of his story. The experienced man might cut the presentation through the sheer boredom of using it continually.

To help salesmen to adhere to a sales presentation at all times, the advocates of visual aid selling evolved a presentation using photographs that were beautifully printed on art paper and assembled in a loose-leaf folder. These aids, with only slight adaptations, covered most forms of selling. The complete story was given on successive pages, each picture acting as a reminder to the salesman of a step in the sales sequence.

Quite a good idea—but is it new? Does it work? It can work quite well for the skilled representative, but it can cause havoc amongst his weaker brethren. The customer is tempted to take the pictorial folder from the salesman, glance through it quickly, and make a decision on the scanty information he can glean at a glance.

And it is not new. During 1936 we produced a similar idea for what was at that time a large sum of money—£400. It was then called *Pictorial Selling*.

The customers don't change

Going the rounds now is another form of sales sequence called the *duologue*. This is a customer participation presentation.

If a buyer is made to feel that he is making all the decisions and is not being influenced by the salesman in any way, an order is much easier to obtain. No one likes to believe that his judgment is being swayed by the selling powers of a representative.

The duologue sequence is built up on a series of sales points. At the conclusion of each major point a main benefit is stressed, such as:

"So you will see, Mr. Brown, that if placed in the centre of your window display it will help sell all your other merchandise as well."

The salesman must then pause, and the customer should reply in words such as: "Well, of course, you are asking for valuable space, but if it helps to move more goods off the shelves, it might be a good idea."

Here is another example:

"I am not claiming, Mr. Smith, that the machine will cut down on labour, but it does eliminate human error. The girls cannot possibly make mistakes, as they do now."

To which the response may be: "There is something in what you say. There are always some of them with aches and pains of one kind or another, and they always blame mistakes on to their petty illnesses."

These two instances show how the buyer is brought into the sale without continually inviting his opinion by such questions as "Don't you agree?", "Isn't that so?", "That's right, isn't it?"...

There is nothing wrong with the theory of duologue selling—but it does not always work out in practice.

Take the salesman who had found difficulty in achieving his quota and visited his sales manager.

"What's wrong with me?" he asked. "I'm sure I'm selling well, but I don't seem to be able to close the orders."

"I'll tell you what your trouble is," thundered his sales manager. "You don't know your sales sequence properly."

"That's where you are wrong, sir," answered the salesman. "I happen to know it by heart. I have rehearsed it so frequently at home that my wife also knows it by heart. My mother-in-law who lives with us is word perfect in it. My two children can recite it more easily than their nursery rhymes—but," and his voice rose, "I haven't met a ruddy customer yet who knew his part!"

When did this happen? Last month? Last year? During the '50's? Not at all. It was told to me by 'Mac', H. C. Baadsgaard, who recently retired from the Board of Directors of NuSwift International.

When did we first chuckle on hearing this story? Why, back in 1937 or thereabouts. Mac, in fact, was the sales manager concerned. And it must have been told hundreds of times since.

There is, therefore, nothing new in the *Duologue Sales Sequence*.

Physiognomy

It has been said that the face is the mirror of the mind. It might be assumed from this that if we learned to evaluate expressions, ear lobes, the cut of a jaw, and other personal traits, selling would be much easier.

Not so long ago we were visited by Morris Pickus, head of Personal Institute Inc., of New York. He produced from his brief case a folder. Like the good salesman he is, he first talked to us about physiognomy. Then he opened the folder. It contained many sheets of paper, on each one of which was shown a face or one of its features—a nose, a mouth, a cheekbone.

Mr. Pickus told us that it had been proved beyond any doubt that men with this shape of nose or that kind of mouth, or this lip, or that eyebrow, could be typed as buyers. When a salesman was taught to carry out a facial analysis, he would know whether a humorous story would be appreciated, whether a buyer was a man with specific preferences, whether he always sampled before buying, whether he was nervous, whether he could come to quick decisions, and so on.

Now that may well be so, but it is not new. We purchased such a reference library of features in the late '30's. We coupled with it another idea prevailing at that time. This brainchild's object was to interpret movement, on the basis that a salesman should judge not only features, but also a buyer's gestures. For example, if his arms were crossed, it was useless to try and close the sale. If he flung them wide apart, then the salesman should bring out his order book immediately, because open arms denoted a readiness to buy.

We launched these new ways to easier selling at a conference but, subsequently, sales didn't increase. We were told in report after report that buyers were not reacting as they should. Salesmen were being mesmerised by their customers. They were spending so much time examining bone structure that they forgot to sell. And far-flung arms sometimes seemed to express irritation, and were accompanied by such words as "Get out—I don't want anything!"

One salesman told us this story:

"I couldn't make up my mind whether he was a buyer who wanted facts given to him quickly, or whether his main interest was sex. It all depended on whether his nose had a ridge half-way up or not, so I kept scrutinising his nose until I heard him say, 'If you don't stop looking at my nose, yours will soon be broken like it!' "

True? Maybe, maybe not. But when the sales force began to treat the study of physiognomy as a huge joke, we decided that it was not for us.

But no doubt these short cuts to success will always crop up and some sales executives will believe that they have hit upon something really new.

Talk yourself into success

I wonder how many people remember the song with a lyric that began "I'm getting better every day". It was quite the rage in the '20's. It came out after a tour of the country by Emil Coué.

Coué was a French psychotherapeutist who studied hypnotism and auto-suggestion from about 1901 onwards. He had a clinic at Nancy.

After investigating the great power of imagination, he claimed that auto-suggestion could cause and cure many illnesses. His famous exhortation to everyone was to say to themselves, *Every day and in every way I am getting better and better.*

No doubt he was a sincere man who did a great deal of good. But G. C. Badouin, in his book on Coué, called *Suggestion and Auto-Suggestion*, made it quite clear that Coué believed that for auto-suggestion to be successful it should be carried out under supervision. He pointed out that it could harm some neurotic people unless there were careful control.

The power of the subconscious mind had a wide influence with teachers. Correspondence courses were started, books written, and lecturers stumped the countryside preaching the gospel that people had only to harness their subconscious thoughts and all would be well with them. We were told that we had tremendous power within us which we had only to unleash to enable us all to become tycoons. However, I have never met anyone who could talk himself into success.

A man must certainly have faith in himself, but that doesn't mean that he can overcome all obstacles. For example, an unskilled after-dinner speaker can tell himself over and over again that he is one of the world's greatest raconteurs, but he will still mumble and fumble and bore his audience when he is summoned to his feet. Skill comes from confidence—and confidence comes from hard study and tough groundwork.

Auto-suggestion still makes a great appeal to tyro salesmen and even, sometimes, to sales managers who have not come up the hard way. Under the guidance of a qualified medical psychologist or psychiatrist, men and women can learn how they can help themselves to health and greater stability. But, in the hands of quacks, the opposite may result.

The untrained psychologist who decides to teach auto-suggestion because he happens to have read a book or two on the subject will never be able to help salesmen to better themselves. They will merely learn how to develop a few more complexes.

An eminent psychiatrist said this:

"The power of auto-suggestion is very great. It is easy, once a suggestion is implanted in a mind, for a man or woman to develop symptoms of many kinds of illness. Rashes can appear, lumps develop, the heart can palpitate, and limbs stiffen. The suggestion of fear can cause trembling and sweating. The power of such auto-suggestion is great, and can cause pain and suffering to strong-minded men just as easily as to those of weaker breed. We know how auto-suggestion can cause these symptoms of illness, but we also know that very few people without a great deal of help can reverse the procedure. Once a fear has developed, no amount of auto-suggestion will alleviate it except under the control of a qualified psychiatrist. In most cases, of course, this is not necessary, as the fears cure themselves as time proves that they were groundless. Or, possibly, a doctor allays a fear, and a pain disappears.

"Auto-suggestion, by itself, will rarely ease a pain. Putting it simply, we can talk ourselves into illnesses, but it is much harder to talk ourselves out of them."

Salesmen were misled years ago into believing that spectacular success could be achieved by harnessing, in some way, the power within them. And what do we now find in the '60's? Why, more books by authors attempting to teach us how to make use of our hidden powers.

Auto-suggestion will crop up again and again in years to come. Someone will be teaching how to succeed by developing this great inner power in the '70's, and the '80's, and the '90's.

We experimented with auto-suggestion for three years. Over a thousand salesmen tried auto-suggestion techniques. We found it of no practical help whatsoever.

Pray for success

Possibly the most nauseating of the 'teach yourself' gimmicks which have spanned the years are the books published for the purpose of proving the efficacy of prayer in relation to success. They rolled from the press between the wars, and they are still being churned out.

Of course, many of the writers are men of integrity and faith and honestly believe that they are helping their fellow men. But others are using prayer as a gimmick, to swell their royalties.

It was said, cynically, in the '20's that 'you only have to pray hard enough and you will wake up and find a Cadillac under your bed.' Someone else said, more recently: "If a few of the men I know who have reached the top got there by prayer, then the Lord has a funny way of choosing his millionaires." Again rather cynical, but it seems beyond belief that, because a man prays to make bigger and better sales, his prayers will be answered. One can pray for guidance, pray for others who are suffering, pray for the light to be given to those who control the destinies of the world. But to pray for a big order? Well, well!

Yet these books are bought and people read about X, who prayed for a large sale to be made, got it, and so began his climb to success, while Y prayed so hard for that million-dollar deal that it came off, in spite of almost insurmountable difficulties.

Will these books help you to become better salesmen? I will leave it to you to judge.

What has changed?

I have tried, in this opening chapter, to prove to you what little change there has been in selling over the last forty years or so. But there has been one dramatic change which, in spite of all the critics, has, I believe, resulted in the salesman's ability today being higher than ever. Those who think otherwise are just misleading themselves.

A Member of Parliament told me that the present type of salesmen who travel overseas can in no way compare to those grand men who opened up the world for British trade.

How ridiculous! Fifty years ago and more, the British industrialist didn't have to go abroad to sell. He could almost demand orders. He set up his own trading stations in foreign fields, and, if necessary, fought off competitors with every weapon in the armoury. But, in any case, there was so little competition to fight. We were then one of the few highly industrialised nations. The world was clamouring for our goods. That was not selling—it was rationing.

If the giants of industry of those days could return to sell now to Africans, South Americans, or the Indians, they would be unable to compete with the selling skills of the French, German, and Italian salesmen. Yes, salesmanship today is generally at a much higher level than it has ever been. When top management doubts this, they overlook the competition of the times.

How, then, has selling improved? The change has been brought about because we are now in an era of management. Large and medium-sized businesses are ceasing to exist as separate entities; with takeovers, amalgamations, and public companies being formed, outlook of management is changing.

British business grew on the back of strong-minded individuals. In cotton, wool, engineering, cars, and armaments, businesses were built up by men who became almost dictators. Those were the days when the major problem was better production—sometimes, any kind of production. Some of the largest companies hardly needed to employ salesmen at all. The boss gave orders, the workers worked, and the buyers queued to buy.

The big change came after the First World War. Many industrialists weathered the storm, although some of them only managed to last out until the Second World War, which gave them a second chance.

By 1946, everything was beginning to alter. With the end of rationing, competition began to grow once more. Manufacturing knowhow was no longer confined to the few. Practically anything that went into production could be copied by British or foreign competitors a few months afterwards. Automation led to overproduction in many factories, and many a tycoon realised that if his company was to continue to prosper he would either have to join up with other tycoons or sell out altogether. The strong and efficient owners of small businesses—the men who, years ago, could have built empires—were faced with the *facts of death*. If they didn't take some action about the payment of death duties while they were alive, then their businesses might be closed down after they had died.

This, then, is the era of big business, but the managing directors, unlike those of the past, own few shares in their businesses. They are, in fact, managers answerable to shareholders, and fully aware of the power of city editors to pull their balance sheets to pieces.

Whereas, in the past, a diehard traditionalist might refuse to have anything to do with what he might have called new-fangled gimmicks—heavy advertising, incentives, sales training, research—this does not apply to the majority of top industrialists today. They cannot afford to miss out on anything. If, for example, they delude themselves with the myth that some men are born to be salesmen, they can find themselves outsold in home and world markets by companies who train their men to sell.

That, then, is the big difference between selling in the '30's and selling in the '60's.

More and more men are being trained to sell—professional selling is coming into its own. This progress will continue.

Our own organisation is used by more than five thousand companies, who send us about six thousand salesmen for training each year. It is doubtful whether six thousand men were given personal training in salesmanship in this country in all the years between 1925 and 1938. It is now generally acknowledged that men can be trained to succeed in selling.

That, and that only, has been the one dramatic change in salesmanship over the last forty years.

CHAPTER II

FARTHEST FIELDS ARE NOT
ALWAYS GREENEST

Are you happy in your work? Let us begin this chapter with that old cliché.

Judging from the number of salesmen who regularly study the 'Situations Vacant' column of newspapers, only a small minority are content with the work they are doing.

We once carried out an investigation into this salesmen-advertisement link, and found that 83% of our sample either examined or glanced through these advertisements consistently. There was no difference between men who had been with their companies twenty years and more and newcomers to an organisation.

Typical of the reasons given for looking at the openings offered by other companies were:

"You never know what's going."

"I was browned off one day and thought I would see what others were offering."

"My wife thought that I could better my position."

"After a few years you are taken for granted."

"I was finding it difficult to sell because . . ."

The majority of men interviewed did no more than look at the advertisements. About a quarter, however, did apply for positions advertised, but either not receiving favourable replies or having second thoughts following a meeting with the advertiser, they had decided to stay in their jobs. Another 10% replied, were accepted, and changed their jobs.

Thus a high percentage of all salesmen make some constant effort to change their employment. Happily for the peace of mind of both sales manager and salesman, employers are not fully aware of it.

When a salesman resigns from a company, he rarely tells his sales manager the true reason. He is loath to disclose that he has been studying the 'Salesmen Wanted' advertisements for a long period. He usually says: "I had no thought of leaving—but this opportunity arose." How did the opportunity arise? The salesman will then give a variety of accounts. He may explain that a friend told him of the vacancy, or that a company approached him, or that he happened to pick up a paper in a train and read the advertisement.

Why do salesmen have such itchy feet? The main reason is that they find selling their particular product difficult, and their sales drop.

There are, of course, other motives. It could be dislike of a sales manager, or a wife nagging her husband that he is underpaid. Perhaps a salesman believes he is in the wrong niche. He may be selling capital goods but believe that he could make more headway in the consumer field. Again, he may feel that selling to wholesalers is much easier than trying to open new accounts with diffident retailers. Most salesmen would be much more successful, and much happier in their work, if they discarded the idea that the farthest fields are the greenest.

Our research division carried out a survey of about 1000 sales executives, ranging from branch managers to sales managers, and found that most successful men had held only one or two jobs. The men who chop and change rarely succeed. This survey was published in TACK Magazine.

A look at different types of selling will disclose to salesmen their advantages and disadvantages.

Speciality selling

Speciality salesmen sell a wide range of products direct to users. Their products cannot usually be obtained from retailers or wholesalers. However, they must not be confused with technical representatives, who may sell engineering products direct to factories for use in a manufacturing process.

Speciality salesmen sell insurance, books, advertising, fire extinguishers, weighing machines, scales, canteen equipment, household appliances (for instance vacuum cleaners and washing machines sold to householders), air conditioning units (extractor fans and heaters sold direct to offices, shops, and factories), cosmetics and brushes (sold door to door), typewriters and other office equipment, vending machines, juke boxes, and services of all kinds.

The speciality salesman is both the highest and the lowest paid of all representatives. He can be the lowest—because he can earn nothing at all.

An experienced salesman may not get a worthwhile position in many branches of selling, but he can nearly always find a job as a speciality salesman. The demand for men for direct selling is insatiable. Because the work is hard, the turnover of salesmen is high. Many companies of this type advertise continually for men, and some must train perhaps 250 salesmen a year to keep their sales force up to that number.

The speciality salesman is always seeking new customers. He rarely has a connection to rely upon. As an instance, a salesman of weighing machines or cash registers may call on a grocer and convince him he needs such equipment, but he won't be able to call back for another order six weeks later. The shopkeeper may need a replacement after three years, but that is a long time to wait for a second order.

Some companies provide leads for their salesmen but rarely sufficient to keep them busy all day. In addition to following up enquiries they must cold canvass. Cold canvassing means calling from shop to shop, from house to house, from factory to factory, from office to office. Behind it is the assumption that if a row of shops contains only one buyer for a particular product, it is almost impossible to guess in advance which shop he occupies. The salesman who tries to guess is nearly always wrong. The only certain way to find a single customer is to call on all the shops. Thus it is sometimes necessary for a salesman to make twenty calls to achieve one or two orders each day. Canvassing can be reduced by obtaining recommendations from users.

The hardest form of direct selling is of appliances and books to householders. It is not difficult to sell them such inexpensive articles as brushes, but an order for a £200 set of books is quite a different proposition.

That is why many door-to-door salesmen adopt unethical practices. In some cases they disobey their employers' explicit instructions, but sometimes firms may condone dishonesty, while claiming that it is not necessary.

Selling direct, whether to shops, offices, factories, garages, or restaurants, can be most rewarding, however. Remuneration is either entirely by commission, or by salary and commission. A salary, when paid, is usually inadequate to meet the weekly outgoings. The main income must therefore come from commission.

A salary, for the speciality man, is a minor consideration. If he does not sustain a reasonable rate of orders, his services will not be kept. Straight commission, or small salary and high commission, terms are unethical and can be considered exploitation unless the following safeguards are present.

1. The product must be saleable at a first call. If the price is £20, the salesman must expect to sell at least five units a week. If the product costs £100, he must be able to average one order a week. If a product is priced even above this and hasn't a quick sale, then the salesman must be given a good salary as well as commission.

2. The product must be competitive.

3. A thorough sales training must be provided.

4. The sales management team must give absolute support to the salesman, by providing him with a sales manual and good sales aids, and by maintaining close contact with him.

5. Sales supervisory staff must be available to give immediate

help to the new recruit or to the more experienced salesman who is passing through a lean period.

Essentially, no company should pay its salesmen by commission only without the confidence that its backing can assure the conscientious salesman an adequate income from his first day with it.

When these stipulations are met, a salesman can generally earn a far higher income through straight commission than through any salary. The top speciality salesmen are the élite of the selling world. Representatives on a more humdrum level may just make ends meet, but the good speciality man can enjoy a far more affluent life—with his own house, his own car, holidays abroad, and good clothes.

Top men who sell insurance, cash registers, air conditioning units, and fire extinguishers, often have executive incomes. The average speciality man can also do well, but the weak man will not be so handsomely rewarded. Incomes vary with the product or service sold. Men selling typewriters, for example, do not earn as much as those selling advertising space or vending machines. As compensation, however, they often have longer to prove themselves and are sometimes given a list of clients to call upon, thus reducing the rigours of cold canvass.

Three kinds of salesmen gravitate towards the speciality field:

1. The man eager to be paid according to his true worth. He is not content to be rewarded on the same scale as other men doing a similar job but without his skill and initiative. The more he sells, the more he earns—and he prefers to be judged by his own efforts.

2. The man who cannot get any other job. But if he is not fired by a similar urge to the man who wants to be paid what he is worth, he is doomed to failure. Speciality selling is not a last-ditch job.

3. The shop assistant, clerk, factory worker, waiter and

others in all walks of life who are unhappy in their work
and want to get rich quick. Again, without the vital
desire to earn what they are worth, they are also likely to
fail.

It is unfortunate that the majority of men entering speciality fields do so for the wrong reason, and then wonder why
they don't succeed.

Background, however, is largely irrelevant to speciality
selling. The top salesmen in four companies have these back-
grounds—shop owner (3), policeman, Regular Army (2),
Navy (2), salesmen from other companies (3).

A speciality man who is successful makes his own security.
He need never worry about the whims of a boss. He is his
own boss, because his services are always in demand. If
there is a slump in trade, his stock rises. Men in other sec-
tions of industry might be dismissed, but he can always get a
job anywhere. He is, indeed, in business for himself—with
his company carrying all the financial burdens. He is in a
similar category to the estate agent, the stock-broker, and the
auctioneer, who also rely on commission for their earnings.
But they must meet their overheads out of it.

"But," argues the salesman's wife, "if a company has faith
in its products, why can't it pay my husband a reasonable
salary?"

The answer to this constant question is that a company
may have the greatest faith in its products but until it is
equally shared by the general public or industrialists, the
salesman is required to turn his prospects' *needs* into *wants*.
No sales manager can tell in advance which tyro salesman
has the determination to make this effort successfully. The
salesman alone knows whether he has become a speciality
man for the right reasons and knows whether he has the
strength and resource to overcome his problems.

It must be remembered that, in the consumer field, some
orders will always be received from a territory even if the

salesman stays in bed late in the morning and finishes early in the afternoon. On the other hand, a firm selling a speciality product will rarely get a pennyworth of business from a territory unless it is the result of its salesman's efforts. A salesman who has the right reasons for joining the speciality field must take care that he chooses a company with which he can progress. He must carefully bear in mind the following pitfalls:

1. Companies that advertise comprehensive sales training may provide only a few preliminary hours in the office of a local manager.
2. Companies that claim enticing schemes which can earn a salesman immense sums of money may be very small organisations, recently established.
3. Companies with little capital, which can often be assessed from the size of an office or quality of sales literature, may not be able to meet their obligations either to salesman or customer.
4. Companies offering unusual 'get-rich-quick' schemes.
5. Companies with products that do not compete in price with similar products of comparable quality.
6. Companies that condone such sharp practices as switch selling.

If, then, the salesman knows exactly what speciality selling entails and its attendant risks, and joins the right company for the right reasons, he can do well. If he is willing to learn a sales sequence and use it at every call; if he is prepared to cold canvass systematically; if he does not crumple up after the first refusal to buy; if he can maintain his enthusiasm day after day, in spite of every setback, then speciality selling can offer him wonderful opportunities.

But a man must have great determination and strength of character to reach the top in this field.

Consumer goods

Men who find speciality selling too hard for them may believe that selling consumer goods is comparatively easy. The snag is, of course, that when selling is relatively easy, earnings correspond to the smaller efforts demanded of the salesman.

A few years ago, many a president of an American company made it clear that in his view the day of the salesman in the consumer field was over. It was accepted that as the retailer never tried to sell products, but merely dispensed soap and toothpaste and instant coffee, a salesman was more or less redundant. It was the weight of advertising that moved the goods from the shelves. This, of course, still holds good, but very few top executives today write off salesmanship. They now realise that the link between customer and manufacturer must be maintained by person-to-person selling. Even the supermarket buying committees can be influenced by local managers who, in turn, are persuaded to display goods by first-class salesmen.

Competition between brands is so keen, however, that advertising alone is no longer sufficient to enable one to out-sell another. There must also be incentive schemes, promotions, and skilled selling to obtain window displays and hot spots on the shelves and counter. A salesman will have little trouble in getting an initial order for almost any advertised consumer product. He can also obtain repeat orders at almost every call. But a good representative will get an increased order at each visit, while the poor salesman will be satisfied with his previous level of delivery—or even miss out altogether.

This could result in retailers running out of stock of a line, and so selling competitors' brands until the salesman calls again.

Often a salesman, calling on a retailer, is greeted with: "I'm sorry but we have to hold over repeating our order for the time being; we still have plenty of stock of X chocolate bars, or Y shoe polish . . ."

Even the most experienced representative would find it difficult to obtain an order in these circumstances. Naturally, he would try to discover the reasons for the lack of demand for his products. He would ask questions like: "*Was your display adequate?*" "*Did your assistants suggest them as extras?*" "*Did you tie in with our promotion scheme?*"

But this probing technique, although sound in theory, rarely works in practice.

A low demand for a product could be due to many causes. It might be poorly packed, not competitive in price, or badly advertised. It might be that the salesman accepted too small an order, and so there was no incentive for the shopkeeper either to display or to push the goods. The salesman could have been a bad merchandiser.

Salesmen rarely fail in the consumer field through poor advertising. If they did, their companies would either have to withdraw a line or go out of business.

Repeated rebuffs to a salesman by shopkeepers not moving his merchandise can be as soul-destroying as the constant refusals encountered by speciality salesmen. For success in the consumer field, the salesman must be a first-rate merchandiser.

Merchandising has been called selling through the retailers. The salesman's first task is to obtain an order and then to sell even harder to be sure of good window, or counter, or shelf displays for his products. There is no difference between selling merchandising and selling goods. The principles of salesmanship apply equally to both assignments. But a salesman who does not apply himself to selling merchandising will fail.

Unfortunately, too many salesmen selling consumer goods lose their enthusiasm after a while and become order-taking plodders. They rarely blame themselves for poor results. They blame these on insufficient or poor advertising. They never tire of telling their sales manager how well their competitors are doing and how superior is rival advertising.

Because commission rates are generally low, these men often lack the incentive to work harder and give that little extra at each call. Indeed, there are splendid opportunities in this field for men who try to improve their selling skills and are enthusiastic merchandisers.

Remuneration for salesmen is normally by salary and bonus, or salary and commission. A car is usually provided.

Before joining a company in the consumer field, the following points should be borne in mind:

1. If the product sold is not advertised, has it such a reputation amongst shopkeepers and the public that it will sell readily? Enquiries should be made of retail shops to establish this.

2. If the goods sold are in a highly competitive market, then it is essential to join a company that backs its representatives with first-class advertising.

3. Is the company forward-looking and modern in its outlook? This can often be judged by its sales promotion schemes.

4. Does the company employ field supervisors or area managers? If not, there will be little opportunity for the salesman to get promotion, as it is rare for a salesman to jump to sales management at one leap.

When a salesman joins a good company in the consumer field, with opportunities of advancement, he must ask himself *Why should I receive promotion?* If his sales do not exceed those of his colleagues he will stay on their level until pension time comes around. Some consumer goods salesmen make little headway because, as time passes, they so often forget to sell. They make courtesy calls at which they produce an order pad and hope to be able to write something on it. They forget that, even if they visit a customer every three weeks, they must find some new angle which drives home a special feature of their product or their promotion. It is because they don't do this that their enthusiasm sags and they bitterly envy someone else in the organisation whose enterprise and determination raise him above them. Salesmen in this field may not have the chances of earning the high incomes of the speciality salesmen, but they have far greater security. Their income is secure, and they are less likely to develop ulcers through worrying about a constant supply of orders.

There are opportunities here for go-ahead youngsters of all ages from 25–55, willing to make an extra effort.

Selling to industry

Although selling typewriters and other office appliances can be classed as speciality selling, the salesman of business systems, accounting-machines, and computers, is in a different category. Usually, his remuneration is largely by salary, and the extra incentives of commission and bonus are smaller. The reason for this is that orders cannot be obtained quickly.

It has been explained that a salesman should work on mainly commission terms only if his goods are saleable on the first or second call. It would be almost impossible to close a sale for a new filing system or accountancy machine on a first, or even a second, call. At the first interview the salesman can do no more than discover the prospect's needs. What problems does he want to feed into a computer? What punch-card system will be necessary, and what information will each card have to supply?

Salesmen who sell costly equipment to industry are usually men with high I.Q.'s Whereas a good I.Q. rating is unnecessary for many salesmen in the speciality and consumer fields, no salesman could, for example, master the technicalities of selling computers or accountancy machines without the ability to absorb the knowledge. Accordingly, companies manufacturing business machines often seek their staff from universities. Their executives visit colleges to lecture; while apparently describing modern office machinery, they are indirectly selling the undergraduates on the benefits of becoming their representatives.

Men with degrees can often earn much more money selling than by becoming school teachers or working in an accountant's office. But most graduates are not fitted for salesmanship, and they should not be swayed in its favour by the money motive. If they decide to become salesmen as the shortest cut to wealth, then they will fail. A man must have an inner urge to sell and a disinclination for indoor life if he is to succeed.

Engineering

This is an extensive branch. Men can sell components to manufacturers, machine tools, welding equipment, air conditioning plant, mining equipment, lighting, packaging, factory machines, plastic mouldings, electric motors, drilling machines, amongst other products and raw materials.

There is a great need for better training for, and more skilful selling by, technical representatives. The problem is one of management. When more managing directors of engineering companies realise the importance of good salesmanship, then representatives will be able to do their products more justice. Very few technical representatives like to be called salesmen. They would much prefer a different title. Many still believe that, as an engineering product is usually bought by qualified engineers, a sales story is expendable. They believe in a straightforward presentation of facts, and the more technical facts the better.

And where do they learn all this from? Generally, from their managing directors or sales directors who may be engineers themselves, and do not understand that in competitive conditions product knowledge is not sufficient by itself to get more orders. Technical men are so obsessed by their knowledge that they often become technical bores instead of good salesmen.

Through inadequate training and guidance a representa-

3

tive may lack both product knowledge and selling skills. He refers almost every query to head office—and rivals get in first, while he is waiting for the answers. As a rule, however, most technical salesmen have sound product knowledge, although many cannot translate the special features of their equipment into customer benefits. Even if they have to sell to consulting engineers or architects, they still have to sell, and not merely catalogue the technicalities of their equipment.

Buyers in the engineering field respect a representative able to convince them that a product is needed and also able to advise and guide them. The first-rate technical representative is a man able to help his customers solve problems. This done, he should sell them on the idea of buying his products rather than those of a competitor.

Because of lack of enthusiasm for selling from both management and salesmen of engineering products, men prepared to combine salesmanship and product knowledge have great opportunities. They must subdue their natural inclination to talk technicalities and arouse the enthusiasm of a buyer by showing what the product will do for him. Those with both skills can rise rapidly.

Salesmanship has many forms

Selling consumer goods, industrial equipment, and engineering products, or selling direct to user—these are the main fields of outdoor salesmanship. There are, however, many other forms of selling.

Consumer durables like domestic appliances, are sold to retail or wholesale outlets. Ladies' wear and men's wear, furniture and materials, are also sold to shops and stores.

Salesmen representing credit traders are often salesmen collectors. They may sell children's wear, prams, or light fittings, and the repayments may be a few shillings a week. They collect the money weekly or monthly, and when the customer's payments are nearly completed, they try to take orders for further merchandise.

In addition to selling drugs to chemists, salesmen persuade doctors to prescribe them as medicines. These highly trained men sell what is called the ethical pharmaceuticals.

Salesmen can sell print or timber, animal foods to farmers or car parts to garages.

Telephone salesmanship has grown rapidly. Men and women are employed to book orders on the telephone, or to make appointments for salesmen to call.

Showroom selling, very widespread in the U.S.A., is increasing in this country. Typical is the motor-car industry, where salesmen in showrooms also follow up leads.

Sales service engineers both service and sell. Merchandisers sell only display or promotions to retailers. There are wholesale representatives, and men sell air travel and freight. The scope of a salesman can be indicated as follows:

A salesman

sells to	wholesalers, retailers, industry, or direct to user.
calls on	buyers, directors, works managers, office managers, proprietors, members of the armed forces, professional men and women, civil servants, farmers.
works for	manufacturers, distributors, wholesalers, growers, and those who market every kind of service.
has an age bracket	usually set between 25–35. Companies operating in the speciality field accept salesmen of almost any age. Men with experience of a particular trade or having good buyer connections can readily find employment between 35–50.

is trained   for a day, or a month, or longer. Sometimes little training is necessary, while otherwise a salesman must undergo rigorous training of six months or more.

can work   by cold canvassing (selling to new prospects every day); calling on retail or wholesale customers every week, fortnight, or month; a small territory may allow the salesman to return home every evening, or a wide area keep him away from home a great deal.

can use sales aids   which may be sales literature, samples, demonstration models, drawings, films, or just a notebook and pen.

and his education   some companies insist upon a salesman having a degree or reaching A Level at school, whilst other companies are little interested in educational background.

can choose   between a relatively secure position with a limited income and few opportunities for advancement, or a high income and the risk of dismissal unless sales are regularly increased.

Many and varied are the jobs for salesmen. But in the final analysis his work is always the same. He has to influence the mind of another person. In his ability to do this, day after day, year after year, lies his ultimate success.

CHAPTER III

HOW TO GET THE RIGHT JOB

Whether an office clerk burns with the desire to become a salesman, or a salesman burns with anger at his company and wants a change, the first step to a new or different position is usually by studying the 'situations vacant' columns. Unless a man can read between the lines of an advertisement he may write innumerable letters without reply, or find himself misled into the wrong kind of job.

Advertisers can be placed in the following categories:

1. Those who believe that good salesmen can be found by making exaggerated claims. The sales executives of these companies are usually first-class salesmen but very inefficient managers of men. Often they lack thorough knowledge of sales management practices.

2. Companies that reward salesmen mainly by commission on sales, that is, low salary and high commission, or straight commission only.

3. Old-fashioned companies that still believe they have only to put their name in print for salesmen to flock to them.

4. The constant advertisers—those with a heavy turnover of salesmen.

5. The 'carrot danglers'—or those offering very rapid promotion to high positions.

6. The economy-minded company whose advertisements are never more than four or five lines.

7. The first-class organisations with highly efficient sales executives.

Let us analyse these various advertisers more carefully.

1. *Those who make exaggerated claims.*

This is the style of advertisement which they might use:

OUTSTANDING COMPANY SELLING TREES
REQUIRE OUTSTANDING SALESMEN CAPABLE
OF EARNING £6000 P.A.

The amounts may vary, but they will always be far beyond the wildest dreams of most salesmen. This type of advertising sets out to attract representatives from other companies, maybe in a similar field. But it usually attracts only inexperienced men, who scent easy money and a quick fortune, or salesmen who themselves make exaggerated claims and change their jobs at regular intervals. The odds against a salesman reaching this kind of income are as heavy as his winning a big prize in a football pool.

2. *Payment by commission only, or small salary and high commission.*

The advertisers may draw up good advertisements but they tend to sell the job too strongly. If a salesman wants a high income and is willing to take risks he will reply to these advertisements. Bold headings are designed to attract attention on these lines:

THERE IS ROOM AT THE TOP
ONCE IN A LIFETIME
WE ARE BOOMING, ARE YOU?
THERE'S NO BUSINESS LIKE OUR BUSINESS
BIG CHANCE FOR AMBITIOUS MEN

Terms are sometimes given as high salary and commission after qualifying, or high basic and commission, or basic plus commission and expenses. The high salary, however, is sometimes given only after a salesman has proved himself on the road. Basic does not necessarily mean salary. It just sounds like it. It can mean a draw against commission. This amount can be adjusted from time to time, and it has been known for a high draw against commission to be cut at the end of the second week of the salesman's employment.

Sometimes the high basic is given only when high sales are achieved. The applicant reading these advertisements must look for a confidence builder. Small and inefficient companies often copy well-designed advertisements from their competitors. The advertisements should be judged by the facts which build confidence. How long has the company been established? Is it well-known? How large is it? Small companies do not often claim to be large international concerns unless they can justify this at an interview.

3. *The old-fashioned company*

There is nothing wrong with joining an old-established company, providing it has progressed with the times. The following type of advertisement, however, gives no indication that a company believes in modern marketing techniques:

*ABCDE LTD.,
REQUIRE A SALESMAN FOR THEIR
POTTERY DIVISION. EXPERIENCE AND
A CLEAN DRIVING LICENCE ESSENTIAL.
WRITE MR. . . .*

This advertisement seems to equate driving skill with first-class salesmanship. Too many tired and weary organisations, once household names, still live in the age when salesmen almost curtsied to the boss. This kind of advertisement reveals that the management has little faith in training and still trusts the myth that 'salesmen are born, not made'.

4. *The constant advertisers*

They may change their advertisements, but the rhythm is always the same. They keep to one theme and it identifies their advertisements:

*WE WANT AMBITIOUS MEN, NOT JUST
ORDER TAKERS*

*THIS IS WHAT WE CAN DO FOR YOU,
NOW WHAT CAN YOU DO FOR US?*

*WE ARE THE MOST GO-AHEAD COMPANY IN
THE FOOD FIELD*

Such sentences crop up time and time again in connection
with particular companies. The jobs offered may be worth
taking; they can be very good indeed. But turnover of salesmen is high, and therefore the applicants must be prepared to
take a risk.

5. *The 'carrot danglers'*

These advertisements appeal to ambition. But although
most men believe they are ambitious, they are not always
willing to pay the price to achieve their goals. The truly
ambitious men who know where they are going do not need
'carrot danglers' to help them on their way. They know they
will succeed only by their own efforts. Top jobs may eventually be available to them, but they will not obtain them
unless they prove to be far better salesmen than their colleagues. The 'carrot dangler', while honestly seeking good
salesmen for future promotion, also wants more salesmen for
the present. The advertisements are designed to appeal to the
men who dream of success, and will often begin:

*TRAINEES WANTED FOR SALES MANAGEMENT
POSITIONS*

Consider this offer more carefully. Firstly, how many sales
managers does the company employ? Two? Three? Four?
Not many companies have more than one sales manager.
They may, of course, employ a regional sales manager,
which is often just another title for district or branch manager.
The average large company, however, does not have more
than half a dozen regional managers. In any case, if an organisation employs two sales managers and four regional

sales managers, it would indicate that it also has a large sales force, possibly a hundred or more.

Why, then, with a hundred men, must the company persistently advertise for trainees for sales management positions? The answer is that, although it is looking ahead to the future, it is also concerned with the strength of the sales force. There is nothing unethical about these advertisements. The advertiser is telling the truth; he is looking for men who can be promoted. But the applicant must realise that his first test is his ability to become a successful salesman. He must appreciate that his chance of promotion depends upon his outselling most of the other salesmen in the organisation. How else can he be chosen for leadership? What can he know about marketing, control of salesmen, sales forecasting, budget control, direct mail advertising, sales training? Surely very little. The company may be prepared to give him management training at some time in the future, but he must first prove he can sell. Until that is established, he will not move ahead.

6. *The economy-minded advertiser*

Advertisements are becoming bigger and bigger. Many years ago a four or five-line advertisement would have attracted some attention if inserted by the right company offering the right job. But when keen competition for salesmen began a few years back, astute sales managers quickly learned that a large response was attained by advertisements with the most appeal, and it was difficult to make a strong appeal in a few lines.

Classified advertisements of 30–50 lines appeared more frequently and space advertisements were also taken in the daily and Sunday press. Most sales executives realise that when salesmen have a choice of a hundred advertisements to which they can reply, the advertiser who has spent most money in attracting their attention and then arousing their interest, achieves the biggest response.

Some very fine companies still believe they can obtain good salesmen by the insertion of a five-line advertisement. But it generally indicates that the company is not up-to-date in marketing techniques. A salesman must ponder this fact before sending in his application.

7. A first-class organisation

How does the highly efficient organisation advertise for salesmen? First of all the sales executive responsible for engaging personnel will take a great deal of trouble in drawing up his advertisement. Draft after draft will be discarded until the final choice is made. This care shows in the advertisement. It is carefully worded, but keeps to basic rules:

1. It will attract attention with a headline or with the opening sentence.
2. It will never be bombastically written, with such arrogant sentences as 'if you can't line up to our standard, don't bother to reply'.
3. It will give facts clearly. If salary is paid, this fact is stated. If earnings are mainly by high commission, then this point is made clear.
4. It will indicate why the company is successful.
5. It will list all the advantages for an applicant on joining the company.
6. It will list the qualities the applicant must possess to fill the vacancy.
7. It will not be gimmicky.
8. It will not make exaggerated claims.

These advertisements are used by companies in every kind of marketing. The salesman who wants to succeed should seek them out. The basic rule for success is to find a good company and then to stay with it.

CHAPTER IV

HOW TO OBTAIN A GOOD POSITION

It isn't true that a good salesman will succeed with any product or service. There must be hundreds who, after being highly successful with one organisation, join another company and fail. They will often find excuses for their failure like:

"They misled me over promotion."
"I didn't like their selling methods."
"Their advertising let me down."
"I couldn't get on with the sales manager."

These excuses are rarely valid. More often than not the salesman does not give of his best because he is unhappy. He feels unsettled. This can happen to an experienced salesman, and it occurs over and over again.

A salesman might be quite content with the work he is doing. He might be selling well and enthusiastically, but his enthusiasm can be dampened by another salesman who exaggerates his earnings, or he can be disturbed by a wife nagging him to improve his position.

It often happens that a salesman selling consumer goods and doing quite well will be tempted to change his job by the apparently high earnings of men in the speciality field. A speciality man who may have been passed over for promotion will scan advertisements for an opening as 'instant' sales manager.

The right way to succeed is to join a good company and to stick with it through thick and thin. If a salesman is successful, there must be opportunities for advancement within his organisation.

Any newcomer to selling, or an experienced salesman seeking a new post, must decide what kind of work he wants to do. It is mere time-wasting to write to fifty different companies in fifty different fields, believing that success could be won with any of them. Too many sales managers also wrongly believe that a salesman with some experience can sell any product without training. The salesman who sells office equipment with excellent results may fail at selling insurance. Having decided the right sphere of activity, a salesman has three choices:

(a) to reply to advertisements;
(b) to write to companies in a field of which he has special knowledge;
(c) telephone or call on companies to offer his services. This may sound enterprising but it rarely works.

The first stage is to write a letter, either in response to an advertisement or to a company who may offer a job. Its object is to obtain an appointment. Most letters of this kind fail in their objective. They are often illegible, verbose, and contain too many irrelevancies.

Your application will be judged by the advertiser entirely by the way you frame your letter. What impact will it make on him? Why should he short-list you? Many letters merely show that the applicants are short on common sense, or that they are parochial in their outlook and have no idea of showmanship or sales promotion. How do they do this? They write on the cheapest quality paper. Here are some rules about this:

1. Never use lined or tinted paper.
2. Never use paper of very small size.
3. Never use paper torn from a writing pad.
4. Use good quality white paper of about quarto size.
5. Personal writing paper can be used if it is a reasonable size, white, and the address is well printed and designed.

In view of the importance of getting a good position and the worthwhile rewards it will bring, the cost of good quality paper to apply for it is very small.

You must either write your application or have it typewritten. Is your writing legible? Do you write in a childish hand? You may be the ideal candidate, but if your letter cannot be read easily you may not get the interview. You may refute the theories of the handwriting experts by being dynamic and yet still writing like a child, but you will possibly not get the interview. The advertiser cannot guess your dynamism. He will get the wrong impression from your hand-writing. Remember, a thousand or more letters may be received from a series of advertisements for sales representatives. When it is hard work to read a letter, it is often discarded.

Ideally, all applications should be typewritten, and it is not expensive to have a letter typed at an agency. It might be costly if several letters were written each day, but this is seldom the case. The man who knows exactly what steps to take to succeed, and sticks rigidly to those steps, will write very few letters before gaining an appointment.

But the right advertisements must be chosen. It is useless for an inexperienced salesman to keep writing to companies who demand special qualities or qualifications he does not possess. He will not get any replies. He should understand that he can only join organisations who recruit inexperienced men—speciality companies, or firms with a training scheme for men without a selling background.

The letter, then, should be typed if possible. Do not try to improve on this and have your biography duplicated. It may seem economical because it can be sent with a short covering letter to many advertisers. But it does not indicate efficiency. It gives the impression that the applicant is writing unselectively for jobs. An advertiser likes to feel that an applicant has specially selected his company. He knows that this is probably illogical and untrue, but he prefers to believe it just the same.

An advertisement must be studied carefully so that all its questions are answered in the letter. If, for example, information of past earnings is wanted, this must be given. If an applicant does not wish to disclose his income, then he should not reply to that advertisement. Too many ignore the request of the advertiser for full information. Here are some true examples:

(a) "You want a good man. I am that man, so just write to me."

(b) "Don't read any other letters. You have found the man you want."

Such short statements rarely receive a reply. Sales executives judge applications:

(a) by the layout of the letter;
(b) its legibility;
(c) the clarity of expression;
(d) the facts given.

Some applicants try to give themselves some business standing by providing the most cursory details about themselves and then adding: "As I do not know to whom I am writing, I will supply further information on hearing from you."

This is wrong. The only possible reason for an applicant not wishing to disclose the name of his employers is that he is afraid he might be writing to his own company if the advertisement has a box number. But if he is writing to his own company, he will be identified anyway because he must give his name and address. Others fear that the letter might be received by someone in the same industry who will pass the information on to his employers. I have never known this to happen.

It is far better for an applicant, once he has made up his mind to make a change, to go right out for the job by supplying all the required information in the first letter. After all, he is no different from a salesman selling his goods. He is selling his own services. No salesman would tell part of a story, and then inform the prospect that he will tell him the rest when he knows more about him.

To summarise: the letter should be typed, should contain all the information required—without spelling mistakes. The following data should also be given:

(a) age;
(b) whether married or single;
(c) details of last three positions held.

If a scholastic background is demanded it should be substantiated; otherwise do not give this information in the first letter. It is the fairly brief letter, with sales appeal, which will get a reply. A letter for a job is no different from a letter asking for an order. The same formula applies. It must attract attention, arouse interest, create some desire on the part of the reader to know more about the applicant, cause action to be taken. How does the letter attract attention? Firstly by its appearance, and secondly by its opening sentence. Most applicants begin their letter with the timeworn "With reference to your advertisement in the . . ."

Surely this can be improved. Here is the opening of a letter from a relatively inexperienced salesman who got the job and later became a sales manager:

"Your exciting and inspiring advertisement in today's *Daily Telegraph* must arouse the enthusiasm of every ambitious salesman who reads it."

Is that hypocritical? Not at all. The advertisement *was* exciting and inspiring. It offered a high income, first-class products to sell, and gave reasons to show that promotion was possible. This letter would have pleased the advertiser who welcomes just praise like anyone else.

Another salesman replied to an advertisement like this:

"Your advertisement in today's *Daily Telegraph* gave all the facts in a few lines. Surely this is the object of all good salesmen—to tell a complete story in the shortest possible time."

Again, this reply did not hint of flattery because the advertiser had given all the facts in a few lines. This salesman got a position. Why? Because the opening attracted attention. It was different from the others.

To attract attention, however, is not enough in itself. It ensures that the letter will be read carefully. But the interest of the advertiser must be maintained. This is done by writing always in terms of the advertiser's interest. Here is an extract from an advertisement for a salesman:

"Our product is a system of storage equipment."

The salesman who got the job created interest in this manner:

"To sell storage equipment must give a salesman endless opportunities. Although I have only limited experience of selling to factories, one point has always been clear to me— they never seem to have enough room. I know of one factory which has a fairly large spare part department and the spare parts are always spilling over the floors. In another factory I have seen containers stacked against a damp wall. Because of this, I know that I can successfully sell your storage equipment."

Here is an excellent example of a salesman writing in terms of the advertiser's interest. Its appeal is far stronger than the standard applications that are the majority.

Creation of desire implies an appeal that the advertiser will find difficult to resist. A few well-chosen words will result in the applicant being invited for an interview. Here is another instance from an inexperienced salesman who 'created desire' in his letter:

"In your advertisement you mention sales training. Of course I am eager to attend. Would it be right for me to believe that at the course you stress the need for person-to-person selling? You would not teach salesmen to try to close orders by mail. This, sir, is my problem. No letter can convey my enthusiastic outlook on selling and my keenness to join your company. . ."

The salesman is talking in terms of the advertiser's interests. He has chosen one section of the advertisement and has turned it into a sales argument on his own behalf.

Finally, a letter must lead to a close, a reply from the advertiser, granting an appointment. Here is one close that brought the desired result:

". . . and I believe in Saturday morning work. I know that this is not possible for many indoor workers but very few salesmen cannot benefit from making calls on a Saturday morning. I do hope that I may bring this extra benefit to your organisation."

These examples show how 'selling by letter' can help an applicant to a sales position. After all, if a sales manager cannot appreciate a good selling letter he is hardly worth working for.

There is one 'don't' which must be impressed upon all applicants. There must be no attempt to write humorously. I have seen many brilliantly funny applications, but I have never known one of the writers to be granted an interview.

When the fullest details are required by an advertiser, should they be included in the letter or written on a separate sheet of paper? If a full background history of an applicant is wanted, it is better to have the information typed on a separate sheet of paper. If possible, however, it should be avoided. The advertiser often skims the letter and does not give the applicant a chance to sell himself.

A letter of a few lines has no appeal, and a long letter is

rarely read carefully. The ideal is that all relevant matter is contained on one side of a quarto sheet of paper. If the applicant's background ties in exactly with the demands of the advertiser, a much more straightforward letter can be written. But this rarely happens. An advertiser, selling watches, would like to receive a letter from a first-class salesman who heads the sales division of a competitor's organisation. Such men, however, rarely change their jobs, and when they do they usually branch out in another direction altogether or want an executive post. The replies the watch manufacturer gets will be mostly from men who have not achieved outstanding success, or who have never sold watches. That is why a good sales letter is imperative.

What advice can be given to the man who cannot write a good letter or find someone to help him compose one? Unless he has a good selling background that will weigh with the advertiser, he must resign himself to writing a stream of letters in the hope that he will strike lucky one day.

It is far better to make a study of letter writing. A well-written letter will get a reply nine times out of ten so long as it is in tune with the advertiser's requirements. A badly-written letter may get one reply in twenty attempts—and then from speciality selling organisations or companies with a high turnover of salesmen.

Anyone who practises seriously and is prepared to tear up dozens of drafts before arriving at the final copy will obtain interviews.

THE INTERVIEW

Your letter has been acknowledged and an appointment granted. You must reply immediately confirming that you will keep the appointment. Few applicants do this, and they may score a black mark before they arrive.

Be punctual

If the time of the appointment is 9.30 a.m., be sure to

arrive not later than 9.15 a.m. Walk around for a while and present yourself at 9.28 a.m., but never at 9.31 a.m. There is no excuse for being late. If an interview begins with your apology for lateness, it is off to a very bad start. The interviewer may pretend not to be unduly concerned at your tardy arrival, but he will be annoyed.

Excuses such as "I lost my way," or "The bus broke down," or "There was an unexpected strike," will not help at all. If the appointment time is for 10.00 a.m., and the train from some distant place arrives at 9.00 a.m., you might consider you have left yourself plenty of time to keep the appointment. But the train could be late. If necessary, catch a train at 5.00 a.m. and arrive at 7.00 a.m., and then kill time as best you can, rather than risk being just one minute late.

Don't make these mistakes

If you smoke a cigarette while waiting, be sure that you put it out when the interviewer asks you into his office. Even if he tells you to keep your cigarette, still put it out. During the interview never offer a cigarette, or attempt to smoke yourself, unless the interviewer gives you one. The salesman who asks the interviewer if he may smoke is chalking up another black mark. The executive might, out of politeness, agree to the request, but he could be a non-smoker and object to others smoking.

If you are wearing a coat or mackintosh, remove it in the waiting room. Otherwise you will go for the interview wearing your coat, and if you are not invited to discard it, you will feel uncomfortable and stiff. If you ask whether you may take it off, you might possibly annoy the interviewer by conveying the impression that you are settling for a long stay.

Finally, do not sit down until invited to do so, and then be sure that you do not adopt a slovenly attitude.

During the interview

If you have taken the trouble to find out about your prospective employers before the interview, you are half-way towards getting the job. So few salesmen do this that those who make the extra effort assure themselves of a good welcome.

When an interviewer asks: "Do you know anything about our products?" he so often receives the reply: "Very little, I'm afraid." How much stronger is the answer, "Yes, indeed, I spoke to a retailer only yesterday who told me there are few service problems with your units and if service is ever needed it is given immediately. You can imagine that made me all the keener to work for you."

Never make the mistake of appearing to be too clever. Some salesmen believe it is efficient to tell the interviewer that they have checked up on his company, that they are aware of the capital of the organisation and the profits that are being made. This is tantamount to saying, "I have had my spies out, so don't try and kid me about your organisation." All you need to do is to find out about the product or service being offered. By all means make enquiries about the company, but don't tell the interviewer about your detective work.

You will not go far wrong if you talk in terms of your prospective employer's interests. Too many salesmen are concerned about themselves. Their main object at the interview should be to display their interest in his business.

Keep it short

Never talk at length about your past activities. Answer questions briefly. Even when invited to elaborate on some event in your past, stay as brief as possible. Nothing is so irritating to an interviewer as a rambling explanation why an education was cut short, or about events in the Services, or how a health setback caused a falling-off in sales.

Never criticise your past or present employers. Many salesmen are too free with their criticism. They begin by saying: "I don't want to appear disloyal, but I am sure you want to hear the real reason for my leaving X." This is disloyalty in disguise. Never criticise your sales manager, or a managing director who once employed you. Never imply that one was unethical, or another drank too much. Never gossip about people you have worked with. Indeed, make it a rule never to criticise in any way your past employers.

Closing the interview

Towards the end of the interview, the executive will have made up his mind about your suitability for the post. He will either engage you or, if uncertain, file your application until others have been seen, or he will turn you down on the spot. To save the face of an applicant, interviewers have set excuses. They will tell him that he has done quite well and must go away and wait until he receives a letter. This persuades many salesmen that they have done exceedingly well at an interview, and they are very surprised to be turned down by letter subsequently. The truth is simple—he did not do well at the interview. There is no other explanation.

When the interviewer tells you that he 'will let you know', the chances are that he doesn't want to tell you outright that you are not a suitable candidate. When he tells you that he will put you on the short list, he is probably telling the same story to all the other applicants.

You can always tell how well you have done when an interviewer does his best to sell you on the job. He will ask you such pertinent questions as when you can start, and how much notice you must give. If you have an interview and fail to get the job, then you have not succeeded in selling yourself. Remember that your initial letter gave most of the facts about yourself, and these facts gained you the interview. Thus you do not fail on facts; you fail because of some mistake at the interview. Check these errors after your next interview and see how many you made:

1. Did you smoke without being invited?
2. Did you sprawl in your chair?

3. Was your appearance untidy?
4. Did you sell yourself with enthusiasm?
5. Did you show enthusiasm for the products to be sold?
6. Did you ask foolish questions like "What about holi-days?" "What kind of pension scheme have you?" or "Do you give luncheon vouchers?"
7. Did you mention that you were also after other jobs?
8. Did you talk too much?
9. Did you show that you were more interested in yourself than in what you could do for the company?
10. Did you produce testimonial letters, battered and grubby, written many years previously?
11. Did you complain about your bad luck in the past?
12. Were you disloyal to your past employers?

Check this list carefully, and then ask yourself how you fell down. Did you try hard to get the job? When the interviewer tried to put you off, did you try to sell him on the idea of coming to a decision in your favour right away?

The first step to successful salesmanship is to be able to get the right job. Such a position is worth fighting for.

CHAPTER V

LITTLE THINGS MEAN A LOT

What are your chances of becoming a first-rank salesman and then a sales executive? The odds against the average salesman reaching the peak of his profession are probably a hundred to one. It may be even higher, for there are no research facts available, but it is certainly not lower. The odds against him becoming a sales executive may well be nearer five hundred to one.

Not very encouraging? It depends on the way you look at it. It offers a great deal of scope to the man who is determined to cut the odds down.

Men who succeed are of no particular type. They could be tall or short, fat or slim, good-looking or less auspicious, fluent or stammering, bombastic or diffident.

Confronted by twenty pupils wanting to become salesmen, it is impossible to pick the one who might succeed. Is it certain that a reasonably intelligent man can become a good salesman? The answer is, categorically, *no*. A man can be trained to succeed in selling only if he wholeheartedly co-operates. This does not apply to salesmanship alone. In the professions many accountants, doctors, and solicitors make small progress. They may have been influenced in their choice by determined parents.

A successful salesman will want to sell in spite of the difficulties, and be prepared to counter them. It is useless to take up selling because of a belief that it is easy, that it can lead to romance in distant places, that expense accounts are high, that it gets a man away from home, that it is a device for dodging supervision, or that it bestows a freedom without obligations to immediate superiors.

Some convince themselves that they want to sell only to find that they lack the stamina to fight for orders day after day. Although some exceptional men can break every rule and still succeed, 99·9% of salesmen must start with certain attributes and, through training and experience, learn to use them.

Although it is seldom possible to pick out men for high achievement in selling, it has become apparent to me over the years that there are certain types of men who rarely succeed. They include the following: men who are overweight; men with long service in indoor jobs like engineers, clerks, and shop assistants; actors; cynical men who believe that the whole world is against them; men with a very unhappy home life; men with very large families; men with hobbies more important to them than their work; men who cannot follow instructions; men disinterested in their appearance; ex-policemen or teachers, who have held some position of authority.

Of course there are exceptions. I know an ex-actor who became a highly successful salesman, but he is the only one from dozens who have made the attempt. There must be teachers who have become good representatives, but I have not met one, although I know many who have tried hard.

Most successful salesmen have either very quick minds or do not know when they are beaten. The average salesman comes somewhere in between.

How can you achieve success if you either lack experience in salesmanship or are making little progress as a salesman? You must change yourself. This may sound radical, but without some alteration there is no reason for improvement in the future.

You need not discover some hidden power. By training, by learning, by casting yourself in the mould of those who have succeeded, by making use of latent abilities, you can change for the better. By finding the fundamentals that lead to success in selling, and by applying them firmly, you can raise yourself above the average.

If you follow these precepts, what kind of success can ensue? You may develop into merely a slightly better salesman. It may bring promotion to branch manager. It may lead to a managing directorship. When a man uses all his potential and arrives at his true status, my view is that he has achieved great success.

If you train yourself to do everything right and finish as a top-ranking salesman, be satisfied with that result. Don't let your ambitions outrun your abilities. You can do no more. You have worked hard and diligently and used all your abilities. If, however, you become a top salesman but have not realised your true potential, you have failed; you might have been a sales manager. It would equally apply if you had reached branch manager status. If that job does not engage your whole ability, you will have failed, because you might have progressed to sales manager. And so it goes on, right through your business life.

What is this hidden potential? As an example, a man may be able to learn foreign languages rapidly, and so qualify as a highly-paid export representative. If he does not use this ability, then he is not realising his true potential. When a man with the stamina for long hours decides to leave early to play golf or billiards, he is failing in his duty to himself. If a man has initiative but keeps it hidden with a 'couldn't-care-less' attitude, he is not using his true potential.

Success is attaining a certain position after using all your true potential. When you reach it, rest content. You have done well. You could do no better.

Research proved some years ago that very few salesmen work to greater than 60% of their powers. Work is not solely the making of calls. It comprises the whole range of salesmanship, from planned calling to human relations.

Some worked hard, but sold ineffectively. Some sold effectively, but made insufficient calls. Some were tactless, and others were grumblers. Some gave good service to their customers, but stopped working too early each day. Many could have been far more successful if they had been aware that they had the power. They needed training and self-discipline.

Look at yourself

What kind of a man are you? Do you boast too much? Do you talk too much? Have you an outsize chip on your shoulder? Do you believe that your lack of success is due to the failings of others? Are you a good listener?

Robert Burns wrote: *"O wad some Pow'r the giftie gie us
To see oursels as others see us."*

Maybe we haven't the insight to see ourselves as others see us, but we must make the attempt. It is indispensable towards training yourself to succeed in selling. You must take a good look at yourself. You must not deceive yourself. We will go through the personality traits and characteristics of a salesman, and his relations with other people, and you should ask yourself at each stage: "Could this apply to me?"

Little things mean a lot

A sale is rarely the result of a sudden inspiration, or a brilliant exposition of a product's salient feature. It is the culmination of a few major developments and a hundred-and-one minor details, all carefully planned towards one end. Everything counts in selling, from the initial hazy idea in a research developer's mind to a huge advertising campaign—and then right down to a salesman's fingernails.

Can grubby fingernails lose an order? It seems ridiculous to suggest it, but they can have an effect on a sale. A dead fly in the shop window of a food emporium could make a passer-by keep passing by. Such an insignificant detail may cost that shop the sale of a loaf of bread or a few cakes. Grubby fingernails must detract from the sales appeal of a colourful brochure or a length of fine material. Clean and well-kept nails will never lose an order.

At our training courses 90% of those attending are irritated by our advocacy of personal hygiene for a salesman. These are the men who have their hair cut regularly and would no more think of presenting themselves untidy, unkempt, and with grubby finger nails, than without their sample case.

But we must advise the remaining 10%. This minority might have one man who had not previously thought about this subject. To him it must be emphasised that a salesman needs eye appeal. He must look right in every minor and major way, every day of his working life. He must not be typed by a buyer. These expressions are often used about salesmen:

"Oh, you mean the hairy fellow."

"Do you mean the one who always looks as though he needs a bath?"

"Oh, the chap with the broken teeth."

The subjects of these comments might consider themselves clean, wholesome specimens of humanity, but they obviously don't see themselves as others see them.

Bad breath causes offence to a buyer. It could be caused by food like onions, garlic, or fried fish. It could have a nervous origin. It may be caused by lack of dental hygiene. Whatever the cause, every effort must be made to cure it, even to the extent of consulting a doctor.

Food like onions or curries should not be eaten during a working day. Neither should beer or spirits be taken unless essential to entertain. Tough? Well, if a man wants to succeed he must pay a price, and these are minor sacrifices. Others, more vital, must be made in time and effort.

A wife will rarely be able to tell her husband if his breath smells, she gets used to it. Have the courage to ask for an objective opinion. If the cause is nervous in origin, little can be done about it. Then a man must always keep at arm's length from a buyer or prospect. Indeed, this distance should always be kept whatever the condition of the breath. No one likes to be breathed upon at close quarters.

Some salesmen never learn this lesson. Only a buyer who can run 100 yards in nine seconds can escape them. They follow closely, breathing directly into a buyer's face.

For many years Lifebuoy soap have advertised with the slogan, "Even your best friends won't tell you." This refers to body odours. I know of at least one case where this problem caused a salesman to lose a big order; the buyer couldn't get rid of him quickly enough.

All of us have been in close proximity to someone with body odour. It might have been a shop assistant, a stranger in a lift, a friend invited to a meal, or a fellow-worker. Each salesman should ask himself: "Could this possibly apply to me?"

Yes, little things do mean a lot—especially to the salesman who wants to train himself to reach the top!

Appearance

Most salesmen believe that they dress well. Only about 60% are right in their assumption; the others are under a misapprehension. It is expected of a poet that he should look a little threadbare. The professor of theology, not thinking of worldly things, may not know whether he is wearing a tie or a bow. A farm-hand would not plough a field in a mohair suit. A salesman must look his part, impressing others as an efficient businessman.

A skilled negotiator, calling on city brokers, should wear a bowler hat and carry a rolled umbrella. The same man would look quite out of place if he dressed in this way to call upon a farm, but he must still retain a good appearance, whatever his clothes. A salesman must be well dressed without being loud or ostentatious. He must be quietly attired so that a buyer receives the right impression. Too many salesmen keep their best clothes for Sunday wear or for special occasions, and use their second-best for the working week. It should be the other way around.

Grey flannel slacks should never be worn by salesmen on duty—but many wear them just the same. They are unteachable. They do not grasp the implications of dressing well. They have the wrong conception of selling.

There is always the exception, a man who does well in spite of a stubbly beard or crumpled linen. But why gamble on being that one in a thousand—the exception to the rule?

What is a buyer's reaction to the appearance of a salesman? Here is the view of an authority, reprinted from *How to Sell Successfully Overseas*.

Doctor Alex Grunther, a leading Industrial Psychologist, gives this explanation:

"*Although great advances have been made in psychology and psychiatry, no authority has moved away from the conception of the subconscious mind. People do not always know what motivates them because thoughts and pictures are stowed away in the back of the mind and are often released only as emotions. For example, the mannerisms of one person could greatly affect another without his knowing the reason. He may believe that he dislikes that person's arrogance and manner, or just the soiled handkerchief which he is handling continually, but this need not be the real reason. It may be something within himself that he really dislikes. This must be so, otherwise the person with the irritating manner would be disliked by everyone; but this rarely happens. His mannerisms only affect certain people.*

"*People who buy are affected and influenced in their decisions by a hundred and one matters. This must never be forgotten by those responsible for marketing.*

"*In its simplest form it could be put in this way: a salesman badly in need of a haircut could influence the decision of a buyer without that buyer ever realising why he had decided against a proposition. It may be that some train of thought has been set up in his mind, a train starting with untidiness which leads on to some form of disgust, lack of security, or lack of trust."*

The modern businessman does not delve as deeply as the motivational researcher or the psychologist, but few would dispute Doctor Grunther's assertions.

Here are some reminders for the man who wants to ensure a good appearance:

Wear a suit, and not sports jacket and slacks.

See that the suit—especially the trousers—is pressed regularly.

Avoid wearing a pullover if possible. If it is essential to wear it, make certain that the tie is tucked into the neck and not allowed to flap outside.

Wear neat patterned ties and socks.

Make sure that your linen is spotless.

Always wear or carry a hat, but never one which is grease-stained.

Don't put bulky objects in side pockets of your jacket.

Make sure that all buttons are intact.

Don't wear jewellery of any description.

Polish your shoes regularly.

You may consider that the cost of being well dressed is above your means. It need not be so. A well-kept yet inexpensive suit will last a long time, whereas a more costly outfit which is badly treated—perhaps just thrown over a chair at night and not pressed regularly—will soon be unwearable. It costs little to press trousers. With the advent of drip-dry shirts, there is no need for one to be worn two days running. Shoe polish is cheap, and so is cotton for sewing buttons. Smart and moderately priced ties are readily obtained in many shops. It is not expensive to dress well, but it may be very costly to a salesman in the long run if he does not create the right impression with his appearance.

Mannerisms

We all have mannerisms. Some men play endlessly with their ties, others pick invisible pieces of skin from their chin. Some scratch the side of their face or drum their fingers on the table, play with a lighter or chew a pencil. If it is impossible for these nervous reactions to be controlled at all times, try to cut them out during selling hours. After all, a member of the family can shout at relations to put a stop to irritating mannerisms, but a buyer does not complain. He may not buy.

So check your mannerisms. Check to see whether any of these apply to you, and if they do, try to counteract them:

Don't sniff.
Don't hold a handkerchief in your hand.
Don't let your lips continuously droop at the sides.
Don't play about with any object on a buyer's counter or desk.
Don't drum with your fingertips on a desk or tap with a pencil.
Don't keep looking at your fingernails.
Don't rock backwards and forwards.
Don't stand with your hands in your pockets.
Don't scratch any part of your face or body.
Don't keep smoothing your hair.
Don't keep buttoning and unbuttoning your coat.

That's enough to go on with. For success in selling you must train yourself to look successful, and to avoid annoying a buyer in any way by your mannerisms.

CHAPTER VI

HOW TO DEVELOP A SELLING PERSONALITY

Have you the right kind of personality for salesmanship? Before you can answer this question, you must examine another—what is the right kind of selling personality?

Some people can only define a sales personality by a salesman who is over-selling. To them a man with the 'gift of the gab' is a salesman. The next stage in this train of thought is that *a selling personality means a salesman who is a fast talker*. This is sheer nonsense. Yet the expression, 'he talks like a salesman' is often used.

Has a loud-mouthed extrovert a sales personality? Not necessarily. Has the quiet, reticent fellow with the winning smile a sales personality? Quite likely.

Generalised views about personality do not carry us far. One authority, Professor McTaggart, observes that "*The self is equivalent to personality and can be known as an object. The self, therefore, can perceive itself as an object of awareness.*"

Is that quite clear?

General Smuts said: "In the personality of every human being there is a unique creative novelty."

Does that make it quite plain?

Dr. Max Scheler wrote: "Personality is a new kind of being emerging in humanity at some stage of its development."

Which sums it up. Or does it?

Under the section devoted to personality in the *Encyclopædia Britannica* the opening paragraph begins:

"Personality is the characteristic way of thinking and acting which identifies each person as a unique individual. Since it is the one psychological concept which impresses all the functions of the individual it has become the basic integrating concept of psychology. Each theory or school of psychology gives a different approach to personality yet all agree in placing it as a keystone in the arch of mental science."

We can read many books, study authorities, listen to words of wisdom from lecturers in psychology—and we still find a definition of personality elusive.

Yet, strange as it may seem, we all know what personality means, without being able to define it. When we refer to a clash of personalities between two people, we know why they cannot have a friendly relationship. When we are told that someone has a grim personality, again we know exactly what is meant.

Our customers understand as little about personality as we do, but they also know what they mean when they describe a salesman as having a likeable personality. A sales personality, then, is one that builds friendship and understanding with the greatest number of prospective buyers or customers. It must:

gain the confidence of a customer;
win the respect of a customer;
win the the friendship of a customer;
indicate to the customer that he cannot be browbeaten.

But a salesman's personality must not:

leave an untrustworthy impression;
antagonise the buyer;
be so weak that a customer knows he can dominate the salesman.

Good buyers should not be swayed by personal preferences, but they all, to a greater or lesser extent, favour those salesmen with whom they have a friendly relationship. It often happens, especially when selling to retail stores, that a salesman calls repeatedly and rarely sees a buyer. The cause

of this might well be that the salesman has antagonised the
assistant who does not even bother to take in his card, or that
the buyer himself has little respect for the salesman. It would
be very salutary if salesmen could overhear the remarks of
buyers when an assistant hands them a visiting card:

> "Oh, not *him* again. Do get rid of him."
>
> "That bore? No, I won't see him—he just wastes my
> time."
>
> "I can't be bothered with him. Tell him I'm busy."

But every salesman believes that such remarks always
refer to the other fellow. A saying amongst salesmen runs:
"He didn't get the order because his face didn't fit." That is
another way of describing a clash of personalities, and it
should not happen in salesmanship. You must often have
heard that "before you can sell anything you have to sell
yourself". What does this mean? It means that you must have
the right kind of personality.

Man is made of many parts and each part forms the framework of his main personality. Many small ingredients go into
the building of the sales personality, once these are built in a
man's personality *can* change for the better.

Personalities do change. An accident can transform a man
with a happy disposition into a morose, bitter introvert. I
know of a criminal who spent many years in prison. He used
to look the part, with shifty eyes and a sneering expression.
Now he has changed. For twenty years he has led an honest,
upright life. He has a friendly and successful personality, and
it is partially due to his devoting a great deal of time to
charitable work. The psychologist, William James, said:
"The greatest discovery of my generation is that human be-
ings can alter their lives by altering their attitude of mind."

How can the mind of a salesman be changed so that it is
reflected in his personality? Quite easily—by developing the
right mental attitude and studying human relations. Successful salesmen must have four personalities that combine into

one. They must have a cheerful personality, a strong personality, a kindly personality, and a sincere personality. Linked together, they form the selling personality.

A CHEERFUL PERSONALITY

Nobody likes the company of miserable or depressing people, least of all buyers. Most of us have troubles enough of our own, without being forced to listen to the ills and misfortunes of comparative strangers. Even members of a family do not take kindly to listening to their sister, or brother, or parents describing in detail their operation, or lecturing on the decadence of modern society. So why should customers want to listen to similar talk from salesmen?

Too many people are depressing. Why should a salesman expect a customer to be absorbed by the illnesses of himself or his family, the gruesome accident just witnessed, the depths of snow outside his house, the rapid spread of an influenza epidemic, his fibrositis or rheumatism or migraine headaches, his children's complaints, or his problems with relatives? The list is lengthy. Of course, some gloomy people relish sadness and misfortune so that they, in their turn, can elaborate on their own complaints. Most of us, however, prefer cheerfulness to dejection, laughter to tears.

Never then, for the rest of your selling life, tell a depressing story or show a despondent view of the world to customers. If a customer starts to depress you with his stories, listen but do not retaliate. The first stage in developing a happy and cheerful personality is to renounce boring others with your troubles. No matter how tempting it is to say "I have a splitting headache," or "I've a shocking cold," resist it. And no one, but no one, is ever interested in whatever operation you may have undergone.

"He is a cheerful fellow" is a very good accolade to win for yourself.

To win complete victory over depression, smile more fre-

quently. Few salesmen smile enough, although a smile can
influence a customer as soon as you meet him. Not a chorus-
girl smile, mechanical as if it had been ordered by a theatrical
producer—but a sincere smile that indicates pleasure. Why
shouldn't you be pleased to see a customer? He is, after all,
your bread-and-butter. Without him you would have very
little to smile about; on his decision, perhaps repeated again
and again throughout the year, rests your future rewards and
prospects of promotion. If you are not happy to meet him,
pleased to convince him that he should buy from you, then
you should get out of selling.

A genuine smile is the universal outward sign of pleasure.
A smile on the face of a child in Tahiti means just the same as
a smile from an Eskimo. A smile takes no account of colour or
religion. It is just as effective from a fourteen-stone heavyweight boxer as from a six-stone teenager. It adds warmth
to life, and it can kindle a spark of humanity in the most
miserly of curmudgeons.

Don't merely smile with your lips. Also smile with your
eyes. Difficult? Impossible? But do you know what to smile
with your eyes means? Think of a time when you have
described someone as having "cold eyes". Did you take their
temperature? Did you prod with your finger to see if they
were chilly? Do you believe that their eyes were physically
cold? Of course not. You were conveying that the person was
a cold fish, someone you didn't like very much. You didn't
take to him, not because he had cold eyes, but because his
eyes gave a clue to his personality.

Clear eyes? Rather a nice fellow. Warm eyes? She's the
girl for you. Sharp eyes? Look out, don't make a slip or you
will be in trouble. People are judged by their eyes—and
smiling ones suggest a smiling personality. So try smiling
with your eyes. Make them cold, then sharp, now warm,
now thoughtful—and now smiling. You've done it? Not so
difficult after all, is it? An anonymous writer summed up the
worth of a smile in this way:

It costs nothing but means much.

It enriches those who receive it without impoverishing
those who give it.

It happens in a flash but the memory sometimes lasts for
ever.

None are so rich that they can go along without it.

And none so poor but are the richer for its benefits.

It is rest to the weary, daylight to the discouraged, sun-
shine to the sad, and nature's best antidote in time of
trouble.

Yet it cannot be bought, borrowed or stolen.

For it is something that is no earthly use to anyone unless
it is given away.

And if in the rush of business a man is too tired to give you
a smile,

then leave one of yours, for no one needs a smile so
much as those who have none left to give.

A STRONG PERSONALITY

Strength comes to a salesman from confidence and knowledge. A buyer meeting a salesman who is unsure of himself
will weaken him still more. Some instinct informs the buyer
which salesman he can push around and which one he must
respect. Years of dealing with a particular salesman may
condition the regard a customer has for him. The buyer will
have learned how to handle him, just as a good salesman will
know how to deal with every type of buyer. The weak salesman will, however, have shown his insufficiency on many
occasions by his colourless personality and his readiness to
accept unfair demands (such as special discounts and deliveries). Buyers take advantage of a weak salesman. For the
weak man to change in mid-career is difficult. If he has won a
reputation for softness and timidity, no sudden change will
alter it. And any change will probably take a long time. He
can, however, ensure that he gives a stronger impression to
new customers.

The young salesman making his way in the world can easily develop a strong personality. He needs thorough product knowledge and must refuse to accede to the unfair whims of buyers. This will not lose him many orders. He must not show weakness by criticising his company or its products. To him it must always be "My company, right or wrong".

A buyer forms his impression of a salesman during the first few seconds of the approach, and he will retain it as long as the relationship lasts. He will judge you by:

Your appearance. Weak men look weak. They wear the wrong kind of ties and their baggy trousers recall Charlie Chaplin in his heyday. The jacket seems to have been made for another. Smartness is a sign of a good businessman, and buyers respect good businessmen.

Your Head. Hold your head high. This will give you confidence. It also prevents that hangdog look which implies that an order is not expected, the greatest sign of weakness.

The way you walk. Never slouch. It suggests a "couldn't-care-less" attitude. If the salesman couldn't care about his products, why should a buyer be interested in them? The brush-off is easily given to the sloucher. Never hesitate. The "hesitator" walks a few steps, stops indecisively, continues for a few more steps, stops again to inspect something or look around. He looks like someone trying to keep up courage.

Never be arrogant. An arrogant walker is a weak man. He tries to look strong when he feels anything but. The strong salesman never slouches, hesitates, or seems arrogant. He holds his shoulders back and walks briskly towards the buyer as though he is not only delighted to see him but is certain he can do him a good turn. The buyer can judge the strength of a salesman by the way he approaches.

The handshake. Don't shake hands with someone you have not previously met unless that person offers to shake hands with you. Some prospects dislike shaking hands with every salesman who calls upon them. If you do shake hands, however, do so in a proper manner. Don't show off as a strong man, by trying to wrench the prospect's arm from its socket. Don't be too friendly by clasping him by the arm with one hand as you shake hands with the other. The "big-shot" salesman sometimes does this, but it is never appreciated. Don't shake his hand as if you were working a pump. He doesn't want his arm to be jerked rapidly up and down. Don't give him a "flannel" handshake. You know what a limp flannel feels like. Then you know what I mean! That sort of handshake takes all the enthusiasm out of your approach. Don't shake hands at all if your hands are clammy. Don't try to wipe them with your handkerchief as you walk towards your prospect. Clasp the prospect's hand firmly, give ONE SHAKE, and leave it at that.

Enthusiasm

The weak salesman is rarely an enthusiast. Most strong men have tremendous enthusiasm for their work and they are not afraid to show it. The weak salesman has some hazy idea that enthusiasm is a symptom of high-pressure selling. Only one thing is more infectious than enthusiasm—and that is lack of it. The buyer who hesitates about placing an order wants his mind made up for him, and the enthusiast can do that. Here is how Stewart Murray, Sales Director of Tack Industries Limited, expresses the value of enthusiasm:

"*Fire in the belly* was how the Greeks described that most infectious of all human emotions—enthusiasm.

"Every man is an enthusiast about something—his children, his garden, his car, or his colour slides. He may not be an excitable man, but note the light in his eyes and the interest in his voice when he talks about his loves.

"Many jobs can be carried out successfully without involving the emotions, but selling is not one of them. A salesman is paid not only to communicate an idea but also to stimulate his prospect to act upon it. It is not enough for him to prepare a beautifully balanced sales presentation. Life and conviction must be breathed into it before it can be expected to make impact. I have known men with a great gift for logical thinking and blessed with intensive vocabulary who have failed utterly as salesmen simply because they lacked the enthusiasm necessary to convince the buyer.

"We British, renowned for preserving a stiff upper lip under all conditions, are sometimes so determined to bend over backwards in an attempt to appear unbiased. This gives rise to the sort of wishy-washing sentence used on me recently by a visiting salesman: 'I think, sir, that if perhaps you go in for this little piece of equipment you might find, as others have, that it will do a fairly good job for you.'

"What sort of conviction is conveyed by such a statement? It is so loaded with half-doubts that it almost constitutes a warning, 'Buy at your peril.' Today we read about the 'uncommitted'. A salesman can never be a member of this fraternity. He is committed hook, line and sinker to his company and its products or services. If he cannot find it in his heart so to be then it is my belief that he should seek a company and a product to which he will wholly commit himself and on whose behalf he will sell with enthusiasm. If he is not prepared to invest this quality in his selling, no matter what the company or product, then he should turn his attention to another type of work, less demanding in its need for self-investment.

"Before he takes this final step though, he should at least appreciate how other salesmen develop an enthusiasm for their selling. They study their product or service upside down and inside out. They find out all they can about their competitors. They become experts on their subject. Their work takes on some of the interest and appeal of a hobby. They become enthusiasts.

"Now don't get me wrong. I am not suggesting that you

should work yourself into a lather of simulated excitement in front of the customer. Enthusiasm is not an act, it is the manifest confirmation of sincerely held beliefs. If you are a quiet man then your enthusiasm must be expressed accordingly, but it must be expressed. Enthusiasm in selling is judged not by how loudly a man shouts but by how convincingly he talks. A salesman without enthusiasm is like a bell without a clapper. He may look the part, but he will never sound it."

To develop a strong personality, be an enthusiast.

Admit your mistakes

The weak man is reluctant to admit that he has made a mistake and will never apologise when proved to be wrong. He prefers to try and justify his error. This weakness is seen by everyone but himself. He believes he is showing strength when he is proving himself to be utterly weak. Weak people try hard to be strong, and they fail by not altering their mental attitude, by not developing a strong personality. They misinterpret the meaning of strength. Some believe it implies toughness, bluntness, bigheadedness, being loud-mouthed, but most strong people have no need for displays of this kind. The man who believes that he never makes mistakes cannot be helped. Strangely, he is always the first to say: "When I am in the wrong, I will be the first to admit it." Unfortunately, he never thinks he *is* in the wrong. Any man who learns to admit mistakes can give himself a happier life and improve his salesmanship. The readier he is to admit mistakes, the stronger he will become. The wise man learns by his mistakes. The fool cannot, because he never realises that he has made them. It is sometimes very difficult to say "I'm sorry," but the repercussions of these two words can be great. Many say they are sorry now and again, but never sound as if they mean it, the inference being that they are taking the blame although the mistake was not theirs. To apologise naturally can be learned. It doesn't require grovelling or whining. You will build an inner strength if, before justifying yourself, you pause to consider whether you are really in the right or whether you are trying to disguise a mistake. During that pause, if you feel that you are in the wrong, smile and say: "I'm sorry, it was my fault."

Don't boast

Because most people want to feel important, even the strong man may talk of his successes to create a good impression. The weak man, however, often boasts when he has nothing to brag about, and so develops the wrong type of personality. He may close an easy sale, but in his account of it to friends everything is dramatised. He enters a dream world. This may inflate his own ego, but it only lessens the regard of others. The timid fellow who would run fast if a girl made advances to him boasts of his conquests. The salesman, fearful of a buyer, will describe how he cut that buyer down to size. The salesman, scared of his sales manager, will tell his wife how he put him in his place. No one likes to listen to the boasting of others. Weak men never learn that the more they brag, the weaker they seem to their fellowmen.

Most imaginative people have a touch of the Walter Mitty within them. They may dream of conquests far beyond their abilities, imagine themselves as heroic and gallant rescuers, see themselves as winners of a Grand Prix. There is nothing wrong with daydreams. They are foolish only if an attempt is made to realise them. Boasting begins in the mind, and before the braggart knows it, he is giving out his imaginary thoughts as the truth. The strong man lets his deeds speak for themselves. The top salesman does not tell others of his brilliance. Someone who is valuable to his company need not tell his customers of the faith his directors have in him. The man who wins the golf tournament at the weekend doesn't bore his customers with his feat. Boasting weakens the personality.

Ask advice

How do you react when someone asks your advice? You may have been consulted about fishing tackle, a stamp collection, gardening, or salesmanship. Doesn't it give you a rather warm glow, a feeling of wellbeing and self-importance? That is quite normal.

If most people are pleased to give advice, why is their help not sought more often? Too many take it as a sign of weakness to seek advice. They would rather be labelled as knowalls. But it is strength, not weakness, to ask the advice of someone competent to give it.

The tycoons of industry would not make a decision without conferring with eminent lawyers, accountants, financiers, scientists, or doctors. That is a sign of their strength. Many a small trader relies on his own judgment and then complains of his bad luck. A salesman should never mind asking advice of a customer on any aspects of marketing and trading—buying trends in a district, buyers' views on packaging, on changes in the locality, on display. A buyer will warm to a salesman who genuinely needs his advice. You always gain strength by having the courage to ask for advice from others.

Criticism

Laurence Sterne wrote in *Tristram Shandy*:

"Of all the cants which are canted in this canting world—though the cant of hypocrites may be the worst—the cant of criticism is the most tormenting."

This sums up the evils of criticism. Those who criticise while pretending to be helpful, are often giving vent to spite. There are exceptions—unimaginative people with closed minds who believe in their divine right to criticise others and that their caustic remarks are welcomed.

But no one likes his critics. Those paid to criticise plays or novels are not thanked by their victims. No statue has been erected to the memory of a critic. Few dramatic or literary critics are objective. They betray their own frustrations, lacking the creative impulse themselves. But their writings entertain. They dip their pens in vitriol, and no one need read their criticisms if he doesn't want to. But paid critics are only a tiny minority of the population. It is we, the unpaid ones, who can do such harm to others, as well as ourselves, by our criticism.

Many hundreds of people come to see me each year for advice. Usually they have problems they cannot solve themselves, and often want to hear that some past or future action is justified. They usually know what is wrong—laziness, lack of ability, lack of initiative, lack of knowledge. But they do not want these weaknesses brought into the open. I do not remember a single one who could readily accept direct criticism. Salesmen and top executives will dispute this, but it is a fact. Here are typical problems raised by visitors to our offices in search of advice, and here are their answers when a direct criticism is made:

(a) Problem: *The turnover of a salesman is falling.*
 "You are not making enough calls and you should certainly work every Saturday."
 Answer: "That is quite impossible. No one could work harder than I do."

(b) Problem: *The sales manager is concerned because he has lost some of his best salesmen.*
 "You are too blunt. No one likes a John Blunt."
 Answer: "I certainly cannot agree with you. I like a man who calls a spade a spade, and so does everyone else."

(c) Problem: *The sales of a company are falling.*
 "You should try an incentive scheme. Why not introduce commission for salesmen, or competition prizes for outstanding results?"
 Answer: "I can't agree with that. Salesmen, like every

other member of the business community, are paid a salary to do a job and they should work their hardest for it. They should not need incentives."

(d) Problem: *A salesman does not find it easy to get close to his customers.*

"May I suggest in the first place that you shave off your beard?"

Answer: "I don't see how that has anything to do with selling. This is purely a personal matter and I don't intend to do anything about it."

These are just a few examples. Hundreds more could be given. So many men asking for advice, and so many men resenting any that is given. Later we shall discuss how these criticisms could have been made acceptable. It must be remembered, however, that there is a difference between necessary and unnecessary criticism.

A man meets a friend who has purchased a new Supercar. This is how he greets him: "But whatever made you buy it? If I'd known, I would certainly have prevented you making this mistake. You should have bought a Splendide—it's a far better job. Do you know the Supercar had a lot of brake trouble last year? I should get it checked if I were you. A friend of mine had a Supercar and it broke down in the middle of nowhere because the automatic gearbox gave out. And another thing . . ."

This unnecessary criticism never profits anyone.

A purchase has been made, perhaps of a car or a suit of clothes or a set of golf clubs, the owner has paid his money and is satisfied with his expenditure. What good can it do to make him regret that he bought X instead of Y? He cannot change it, he will have to live with it, so why not leave him feeling happy with his lawn mower or do-it-yourself television kit?

If we cannot help other people, then we should not harm them. Dissatisfaction with a purchase can cause misery. Make it a rule, therefore, never to criticise for the sake of criticism. Remember also that when a friend invites you to criticise, he doesn't really want it; he is asking for your praise.

When you ask someone:

"What do you think of this pen?"
"What do you think of my roses?"
"What do you think of this snap I took in the South of France?"

Do you want these answers:

"That's about the worst pen on the market."
"You must have pruned badly. They are much too small."
"Why don't you learn to take a decent picture and stop kidding yourself you're a first-class amateur photographer?"

Or do you want these answers:

"A very good pen, that."
"A lovely rose."
"That's a good snap—let me look at it again."

Judge for yourself.

There are times when you must criticise, occasions when it is essential to explain carefully that a mistake is being made or that disaster looms ahead if a course of action is not altered. But before pointing this out, you must be convinced that there is no alternative.

Judges can criticise witnesses or barristers; teachers may criticise pupils; sergeant-majors can criticise raw recruits. They, and others in authority, may be disliked for their criticism, but the nature of their responsibilities demands it.

Life would be simple if all criticism were acted upon. It would benefit those John Blunts who find it hard to believe that no one appreciates their verbal thrusts, but that they inspire respect.

Some John Blunts are kindly, with a love for humanity that makes their bluntness acceptable—but they are few and far between.

My impression of a John Blunt will change when I meet one who can take bluntness in return. They may be rude and direct themselves but if anyone answers them in the same way they get angry and their blood pressure soars. When someone is praised in such terms as "I like him. He's direct and blunt—a good type," it usually follows that he has been blunt, direct, and critical towards everyone but the person making the statement.

How can essential criticism be made palatable? One way is to temper criticism with praise, and another is to place yourself in the position of the person being criticised. Let us apply these principles to the problems raised earlier in this chapter:

(a) *A salesman's turnover is falling*

"Let me tell you how I once solved a similar problem myself. I felt that I was selling well, and you have assured me that you believe you are selling as well as ever. Yet my sales were not high enough—and the same applies to you. That is why you are here. A friend suggested to me that I should try to work out how I could make more calls, because, as he rightly explained, there is a direct relationship between calls and sales. He even suggested that I should work on Saturday mornings. I thought that a huge joke at the time. But something had to be done, so I took his advice and found that I could average two calls extra every day, and two calls on Saturday mornings. Sales began to rise, so let us see how we can get some extra calls in for you. . ."

(b) *Bluntness that intimidates sales representatives*

"The fact that you are here for advice proves that you are one of the few ready to take the blame if it is just. Sometimes, we must subdue our natural inclinations to avoid hurting other people, and salesmen, even the tough ones, are very sensitive to criticism. Because you are a strong man, I am sure you will take my advice. Weak men are afraid of not appearing to be strong, and compensate by throwing their weight about. When you and I were salesmen we may have accepted bluntness easily, but most men do not. A salesman has to save his face. Your problem is so typical, and I know that you will be able to solve it as others have done . . ."

(c) *Company sales falling*

"You wouldn't have grown into one of the largest companies in your field if you had not always been ready to accept advice. Well, here's an old and tried method which I am sure you will readily adopt. It is an incentive scheme to get your salesmen to sell more . . ."

(d) *The salesman who could not get on with people*

"Your beard suits you. I once grew a beard and got quite attached to it, but for some strange psychological reason, a few of my customers seemed to object. I remember having many quarrels with well-intentioned friends and relatives who told me to shave it off before I agreed that they might be right. It took me a long time to get over it. It shouldn't take you so long. Take my advice and become clean-shaven again. You have a good enough personality without having to decorate it."

In fact, I did once grow a beard. I did once waste time when I should have been making calls. So my advice was truthful. But if a personal experience cannot always be provided, an instructive comparison with another can show how a problem was faced and overcome.

Remember, then, to criticise only if it is essential. And if you must criticise, ensure that it is acceptable.

A strong personality is built upon a determination to win

respect by acting towards others as you would have them act towards you.

A FRIENDLY PERSONALITY

You can check whether you have a friendly personality. How do your buyers' subordinates react to your visits? A shop assistant, a worker at a bench, a foreman, or a typist can undo all the good work that a salesman has put in with a buyer. The salesman without awareness and a friendly personality may wonder why he misses so many orders. An order has been promised, it has only to be countersigned and posted, but it does not come, and the salesman wonders why. It often happens that some assistant has changed the buyer's mind.

The salesman who puts on an act of friendship may deceive a buyer and his assistant for a time, but, like all acts, it will be seen through in the end. Assistants, in all businesses, know instinctively which salesmen have friendly personalities and which are only making a pretence of friendship. If a salesman is met with cordiality by everyone, from the commissionaire to the managing director, then he has a friendly personality. And it is not acquired by sycophancy or flattery.

A friendly personality does not include switching on the charm, or being ingratiating, using stock expressions like 'old boy' and 'old man'. It is a personality that radiates warmth and friendship. A dictionary definition of friendliness is *'attachment from mutual esteem'*. When the salesman wins the esteem and friendship of the buyer, selling becomes so much easier.

Don't be funny

You don't win friends by being known as a 'funny man'. Except maybe after a few drinks in a pub, few people appreciate a string of funny stories, one is enough. Others in the gathering are too intent on telling their own favourite anecdotes.

6

Very few top business men tell story after story. It is the lesser men eager to attract attention to themselves who begin: "Have you heard this one?" It is their only chance, if only for a few fleeting seconds, to capture the limelight. The more stories a man tells, the more boring he becomes.

Television presents the cream of the world's comedians—men who devote their lives to making others laugh and have highly-paid script writers to feed them with matter and patter. Even so, seven out of ten of their stories fall flat. Some hardly raise a ripple of laughter. Yet many men—especially sales-men—consider they are good at telling funny stories. They have only to remember how they feel about the stories told to them to appreciate how theirs are received.

Take no notice of the laughter after one of your stories. It is often forced and unreal. Only the exceptional story told by the exceptional story-teller is worth hearing.

You do not develop a friendly personality by telling funny stories. Listen attentively to others, but refuse to retaliate.

Remember names

We all like a man who remembers our name. We dislike the person who mispronounces our name and we have little regard for anyone who calls us "Mr. Er . . ." or "Mr. Um. . ."

Frank Case said, "I think it humanly impossible for anyone to think of his own name as a word of little importance." But many salesmen do not bother to find the names of prospec-tive buyers before calling. How proud the average person feels when a head waiter greets him by name. The housewife preens herself when, after one visit to a shop, the assistant remembers her name. A buyer reacts in the same way.

Here is an approach that a salesman might make:

"Good morning, Mr. Johnson, it is good of you to spare me your time. This is how we can cut down waste, Mr. Johnson. Just look at this . . ."

Read that aloud. Read it again, but leave out Mr. Johnson's name. It doesn't sound the same, does it?

For a friendly personality, you must always remember the other person's name—the names of shop assistants, garage hands, secretaries, and, of course, buyers.

Here are some rules to guide you in remembering them:

1. You cannot remember a man's name if you are more interested in what you have to say than what the customer wants to hear. Be interested in him. Think of him as a personality. If you want to remember his name, you will.

2. Write down the names of your customers and prospective customers—anyone who can help you to get an order. Do it immediately after leaving the shop, office, or factory. Refer to your diary every time you call on that customer so that you get his name right.

3. Make certain that you know how to spell a name. When you ask a shop assistant for a buyer's name, don't be satisfied with a gabbled answer. Mr. McPherson could sound just like Mr. Mackeson. Mr. Lemm can sound like Mr. Lamb. Ask the assistant to spell the name, and then spell it back to make sure that you have it correctly.

4. Use the buyer's name at least seven times during the sales presentation. Repetition will help to fix it firmly in your memory.

Friendship begins when you remember a man's name.

Your voice

Salesmen need not be orators or spell-binders. They need not have that deep-brown voice we admire in Shakespearean actors. They need not have an Oxford or Cambridge accent. They must, however, have the friendly voice that goes with a friendly personality.

To be a first-class public speaker may well be beyond the

powers of a salesman. After all, it is beyond most men. But he must know the value of the voice and its effect on his personality.

A rasping voice can irritate a buyer.

A monotonous voice can bore a customer.

A loud voice can deafen a prospect.

A quiet voice will please both prospect and customer.

Is your voice shrill, or pitched too low? There is only one way to find out. Get hold of a tape recorder, and record the voice of an exceptional speaker, a lecturer on the radio, for instance. Then record your own voice. Listen to both, and make an honest appraisal.

Improving a voice is both long and arduous. You may go to evening classes where voice production is taught, or you may need only slight assistance. Constant practice can make great improvement.

One of the finest speakers in this country, and also one of the best teachers of public speaking and voice production, is J. H. M. Whitton.

Here is the advice he offers to the man who wants to improve his voice:

"If you will use four suggestions every day I can give you a guarantee that the use of your selling story will improve by at least 20 per cent in one year. But you must practise each one of these in some way regularly every day.

"The first of my suggestions, or signposts to success in speaking, is this: practise deeper breathing every time you use words, so that every time you use speech you have the right amount of motive power behind the words to carry them to their destination. It doesn't matter whether you are selling, saying 'good morning' to the family, or asking a woman to marry you, you must have enough force behind your words to finish them effectively. Even in everyday conversation in the train or the bus, make deeper breathing for better speaking a subconscious habit.

"My second suggestion is one of the easiest of all tips to put into actual practice, but I know from experience and from the lives of many people who are interested in the subject of better speech that this suggestion will help very materially.

"Take ten minutes every day and spend that time reading aloud. This can be done from any kind of written material, but naturally it is wiser to use journals, newspapers and books that provide well-written English.

"If you like, take the Good Book. Quite apart from its theological significance, the Bible is full of magnificent language. It is filled with fine reverberating authoritative words. These will enable you, as a user of words, to overcome the fear of your own voice. This is possibly the greatest obstacle of all to progress in the art of speaking and once this obstacle has been surmounted progress in the use of words will be fast indeed.

"Read aloud every day, listening, as you become used to the exercise, to the cadences and rhythms inherent in all normal voices. You will be astonished, I am certain, at the difference this simple exercise will make. Obviously, if your family will allow you to read aloud to them, then you have a ready-made audience. If they will not allow you to do this, do not be deterred. Go to the bottom of the garden, or out into the nearest park and do the work there!

"Thirdly, try to add one new word every day to your vocabulary. In the reading you do, find one word you are not quite sure about and check its meaning in your dictionary. Thereafter, use it actively and you will find quite quickly that your power of expression—the power to describe your goods and services—will become richer and much more effective. At the end of a year you will have added to your word power and to your selling power.

"Fourthly, while you are practising the control of breath and reading aloud, practise what all speakers seek for— the power of projection, or 'forward speech' as it is very often called. This means the power to start your words as far away as possible from their birthplace when they start on their journey to your listener. Very often words are almost stillborn because the speaker does not practise 'forward speech'.

"You can practise forward speech, or projection, very easily every day, every time you open your mouth to speak. It can be done as a mental exercise and it doesn't demand a very great deal of application once you become used to the idea. Imagine that the words you are making and using are coming from a point where the top teeth and the hard roof of the mouth meet. Begin to push your words out from there—imagine they are starting from a point about a foot or eighteen inches in front of your face. This is a continuation of the first stage at the front of the mouth. After you are used to this exercise (if you are really enthusiastic), go into a room, the larger the better, and select a point at the back of the room: better still ask a friend to sit there—it is more helpful to speak to a face than to a point, and speak to that point or face. Naturally, at the same time you will use the second of the projection points from which you are launching your words. You will be surprised, agreeably, how easily and rhythmically your words will begin to move towards the distant point. At this juncture you will start to achieve the ultimate goal of all speakers—forward speech, an aid to fluency. Remember, fluent speech represents clear thinking, and speech and thought working harmoniously together can mean so much more for the success of your sales story."

Right at the heart of all the work we do is what we have already called good delivery. This means expression of ourselves. Expression of ourselves means how we feel about our job, our product, our company, indeed, all that we do in life to make it worth living. Good delivery, the exciting and colourful use of words, really means the expression of personality.

Expression of personality has been called good selling. So good delivery—good use of words—really means good selling, and better delivery—better delivery of words—means better selling. I cannot imagine that any of us, involved as we are in the art and craft of salesmanship, would not look every day for the means to improve our professional skills—and sales effectiveness.

To develop a friendly personality, improve your voice.

Tact

"No man with prejudices should ever be sent abroad to sell."

These words were used by an export director. He went on to explain that anyone with race or religious prejudices would inevitably reveal them at some time or another, and thus lose orders and, more important, goodwill.

This is true. I have been in many parts of the world and heard of orders lost through the tactlessness of export representatives. The man with strong prejudices usually lacks tact. But tactlessness is not exclusive to this kind of man. Unimaginative people are often tactless because they do not know they are hurting others. We all make tactless mistakes at some time or another and wish that we had bitten our tongue instead. If we are conscious of this weakness, we can reduce it to the minimum, although we cannot always entirely eradicate it.

To the prejudiced, little advice can be given. They must cope as well as they can with their mixed-up outlook. To the unimaginative, little help can be given. If a man does not know he is doing wrong, how can he be cured of his faults? But most of us can learn to be more tactful.

Here are a few rules.

Men of all nationalities, colours, and creeds can tell stories against themselves and enjoy them. They do not, however, relish the stories of others about their so-called characteristics.

Never make sweeping statements like, "*I can't stand Frenchmen*," or "*Australians get me down*," or "*Americans are a pain in the neck*." You may have disliked an Indian you met, or perhaps a Dutchman has annoyed you, but only a fool would condemn a whole nation because he disapproved of one or two of its people.

Find out more about people before jumping to conclusions. I was with a woman who produced a photograph, apparently of herself with her husband and daughter. Immediately, another person looking at the photograph said: "Is that your daughter? Doesn't she look like you?"

Well it wasn't the daughter; it was the wife's sister, a girl of about nineteen, and the couple were much too young to have a child of that age. This was an utterly tactless remark that could have been avoided with the question: "And who is that?"

Do you want to know whether you are tactless? Ask yourself if you have ever greeted anyone with:

"You're not looking too well!"

If so you're tactless.

You can change merely by not hurting and upsetting people. To develop a more friendly personality, be tactful.

Courtesy

Do you believe equality of the sexes makes some of the past courtesies towards women irrelevant?

You don't believe that? Good! Then check this list:

1. Do you always raise your hat when greeting a woman?

2. Do you give up your seat in a train or bus for one? Not offering a seat to a lady is not excused because you made the offer once and it was refused.

3. Do you elbow your way to the front of a queue, pushing aside any girls who may be waiting?

4. Do you take off your hat if a lady is in a lift?

5. Do you open the door for a woman customer in a shop and step aside to let her pass?

6. Do you help your wife or girl friend into her restaurant seat before you sit down?

7. Do you stand up if any acquaintance approaches your table?

8. Do you thank everyone for their service—the waitress, bus conductor, and shop assistant?

9. Do you reply to invitations and letters by return of post?

10. Are you as courteous to your family as to strangers?

This list is not exhaustive, but it is sufficient for you to check your standard of courtesy.

There is no half-way house in courtesy. Confucius said:

"If we could all be courteous for even a single day the hatreds of humanity would turn to love."

Try it first for one day, and then maintain it thereafter.

Giving praise

Flattery is no part of a friendly personality. No one wants a friend who always lies, and to flatter is to lie. The fifty-year-old lady buyer who looks sixty is not taken in if she is told she looks thirty. She may seem flattered, but she knows it is a lie. But if she could be mistaken for a woman in her early thirties, she cannot be reminded too often. It is the truth, and she knows it. Her mirror proves it.

People are not charmed when they see through flattery and know it is false.

On the other hand, few people give praise and appreciation where it is due. Husbands find it hard to praise their wives, and wives are tongue-tied at the thought of expressing their appreciation of their husbands. The managing director won't praise his executive team, the executive team won't praise the office manager, the office manager won't praise the staff, and the staff won't praise anyone. Too many sales managers find it easier to criticise a salesman than praise him, and many a salesman would rather blow his own trumpet than raise the self-esteem of a customer by praising his display, advertisement, or factory layout.

Why is this? I do not know. Some people will not praise for fear of being thought flatterers. But most are just pig-headed. Praise can make others happy and, if it is withheld, it can turn a warm-hearted person into a sour cynic.

General Smuts said: *"Praise can bring colour to the drabbest of lives. It can make life worth living, and help a man to succeed."*

It can work wonders for the giver and the recipient. It is as welcome to the successful as the unsuccessful. When a chairman is praised by a City Editor for the fine results of his company, he glows with pleasure. I was with one who was singled out for this reason in a leading newspaper; he insisted on ordering champagne all round. But normally he counts every penny he spends. Would he ever praise another? Never.

I have seen tough newspaper columnists made very happy indeed by praise for their writing—and these are men who like to think of themselves as cynical and hypercritical, never taken in by flattery. But they were delighted by praise they knew to be deserved.

Those who complain bitterly that no one appreciates their efforts are the very people who do not give praise in return.

How often have you heard such remarks as:

"He doesn't appreciate me."

"They don't appreciate me."

"They don't know what I do for them."

"They are never satisfied."

"You can kill yourself for him before you get a word of praise."

"He's always grousing, but never gives a pat on the back."

These are typical of people starved of praise. How do you react when someone praises you for work well done? Do you feel annoyed? Do you lose your temper with them? Of course not. You feel all the better for their kind words.

Constant criticism kills ambition, but praise boosts a man's self-esteem and everyone needs to feel important. Praise everyone who gives you good service. Praise the shop assistant who takes pains to help you. Praise the driver who drives well. Praise the little people. Praise the big people. Praise your customers. Praise your executives. Praise your family. But the praise must be merited and the appreciation honest.

Only the strong man can praise others. The weak man is often niggardly in his praise because he feels that, if he gives it, others will ask favours of him. Praise does not make a man swollen-headed; it helps him to do even better in the future than he has done in the past.

Of all the thousands I have met in a long business career, none failed to respond to justifiable praise. Our enemies flatter us, but our friends praise us only when they believe it is honestly deserved. That is why justifiable praise and a friendly personality are linked.

Look and see

How observant are you? Many people look, but see little. The flicker passing across the face when something distasteful is said; the change of expression in a waiter when some buffoon snaps his fingers to attract his attention; the fear in a child's eyes as adults mention gruesome details of an illness; the glint of anger at some tactless remark; the attempt at bonhomie as a disguise for anxiety—only observant men notice these signs and can tread warily by changing the topic of conversation or giving help where it is needed. It is a standard joke that no husband ever notices his wife's new hat or hair style. How many family quarrels have been caused by such a failure of observation? Women are usually much more observant than men. Men should strive for more equality of the sexes in this respect.

This letter shows the value of observation:

"It was a difficult interview. I had noticed when I came into the room that he had a book on archaeology on his desk. When the conversation got bogged down, I seemed to knock the book on to the floor by accident. I picked it up, apologised, and glanced at the title. Then I admitted my own interest in archaeology, which had begun when I was in South America. And we got on like a house on fire..."

Would you have noticed that book, or would you have been so self-absorbed that such details would have escaped you?

Before going into a shop, look at the window so that you are familiar with its display. In an office, look for a sign of a hobby, or for a family portrait. In a factory, look at the lay-out, and the employees. What you observe can help you to get on better terms with the buyer. Notice little things— badges, regimental ties, nicotine-stained fingers. Notice big things—automation, air-conditioning, fork-lift trucks. Observe everything from inter-office telephone systems to the demeanour of a secretary when she arrives with a message for her chief.

When you are observant, you can talk in terms of the other man's interests. You can discuss his likes and dislikes. You can give praise when it is due. You can avoid making tactless remarks. Is it hypocritical to develop a friendly personality? Think of it this way: is it hypocritical to be courteous to those who help you? Is it wrong to make people happier by showing appreciation for their actions? Is it wrong to respect all the little people who go into the making of a big business?

Your answers to these questions must show that far from being hypocritical, it is good to develop a friendly personality.

A SINCERE PERSONALITY

About 350 B.C., Mencius said: "*If Heaven wishes that the kingdom should enjoy tranquillity and good order, who is there beside me to bring it about?*" And this he set about doing. For more than twenty years he travelled from court to court in China, to lecture and even ridicule men in high places. He believed in the principles of benevolence, righteousness, and piety, and the judgment of conscience. He said: "*There is no greater delight than to be conscious of sincerity and self-examination.*" To search our own souls and find that we have not been motivated by jealousy, envy, and unkindness, that we have acted with sincerity is, indeed, a great satisfaction. Sincerity means being genuine, free from prejudice, the same in reality as in appearance. To look sad on hearing bad news but to be secretly delighted at another's misfortune is the height of insincerity. Both to appear and to be concerned is to be sincere. For a sincere personality you must pursue an ideal. You must be different from others, who are insincere without knowing it.

There are signposts to guide you towards a sincere personality.

Don't be a gossip

How can a man be considered sincere if he gossips about anybody and everybody? The man who refuses to add fuel to the fire of rumour and avoids denigrating someone on hearsay evidence is sincere. Only a man of strong character can stand aside from a bunch of educated savages when they tear to shreds the character of a close associate. It might be asserted that a man is a homosexual, but who knows this for sure? Who found him in a compromising situation? Whom did he tell of his weakness? These questions cannot usually be answered. Someone has started a rumour; it has been circulated and made the subject of gossip. Even men of intelligence and honour will often forget their friendly relationship with a colleague and help the mudslingers.

Why are rumour-mongering and gossip insincere? Because any gossip will meet the subject of his rumours and greet him with normal friendliness. He makes a pretence.

The man who ignores a friend he has condemned on flimsy evidence may be wrong, but at least he is sincere.

The next time when you are amongst a crowd of gossips, refuse to take part. Stand up for the person who is the target of the gossip. Most of them will admire you for your sincerity.

Don't gossip about your company executives.

Don't gossip about your colleagues.

Don't gossip about your customers.

In fact, don't gossip. Be dependable.

From dependability develops sincerity. When our conscience tells us that we have not let a customer down, we are free of pretence. For we might, in our eagerness for a sale, have offered to deliver display material the following day, without any certainty that the promise could be kept.

Many salesmen, however, ease their consciences by giving themselves excuses. "The showcards are useless without the goods—and they won't arrive for three days." But the promise was for the next day. "I forgot that I had to go to London." But the promise was made for the next day.

No excuse condones a salesman who breaks his word. If there is an urgent reason for not keeping a promise, illness perhaps, then the customer should be telephoned immediately and told what has happened. There is no substitute in selling for dependability.

To be reliable you must keep all your promises, both big and small.

"I'll send you a card." Then send the card.

"I'll telephone you when I'm in town." Then telephone.

"I'll recommend it." Then recommend it.

"I'll arrange a date later." Then arrange the date.

Keep your temper

Can you be relied upon if you lose your temper easily? When temper is lost, reason goes. Without sound reasoning, a man might make a false statement that causes harm, inconvenience, or loss to a colleague or business associate. A man with a bad temper is often undependable.

It is fashionable for psychologists to urge us to give vent to tantrums now and again—to yell, to shout, to bluster, to complain. When it has all blown over, they say we shall all feel much better for having cleared the air.

It isn't true. After a flaming row, most of us don't feel better; we feel remorse for our loss of control. Only simpletons will feel better, because they do not perceive that they have hurt someone. They are so sure they are in the right.

But is it morally right, after losing one's temper, to say: "Ah, that's better! I got it off my chest and feel a different man." The other man is feeling much worse for your bad temper. You may have made his life un-endurable.

This often happens. "But", say the psychologists, "it will do you harm to bottle it up. You will get ulcers."

Who gets the ulcers? The man who blasts off or the man at the receiving end?

Equals can lose their temper with one another. That's fair enough, provided nothing is said in the heat of the moment that may affect their relationship for years afterwards. But most people lose their tempers with someone who cannot answer back—a manager, a member of the staff, a bus conductor. The managing director rails at his sales manager; a salesman ticks off a shop assistant for failing to transmit his message to a buyer.

They believe they have right on their side, but this is not sufficient. The man who loses his temper wins only a temporary victory. Whom would you rather have as your counsel in court—the calm, decisive lawyer, or one who might lose his temper with judge or witnesses?

Are you pleased when a footballer loses his temper on the field and strikes another player? What do you think of a policeman who, suspecting you of a motoring offence, loses his temper when you deny it? Do you rate highly the politician who loses his temper on TV? Do you feel embarrassed when someone in authority shouts at a subordinate in public?

Few people gain in stature from losing their temper. We shouldn't be human if, now and again, we did not blast off, but it is far better to be known for an even temper than for being temperamental.

Honesty

There are no degrees of honesty. You are either honest or you are not. Many, however, are unwittingly dishonest. Men who would shrink with disgust at the thought of keeping a purse they had found on a bus would get off without paying their fare if a conductor did not approach them. Someone once said that the only honest men were those who did not need to be dishonest. This is not true. Many become more honest as they grow older, but usually because they are wiser with age. Most people are very honest, and only err through ignorance.

A secretary may not consider it dishonest to remove one of her employer's pencils. But it is still theft. Thousands who would be offended if accused of dishonesty pilfer from their places of work. They may occasionally take home a few screws for a do-it-yourself job, an odd piece of wood, or a few lengths of wire, but this is dishonest. A salesman or a sales manager who puts cigarettes on an expense account without a proper reason, or inflates a luncheon bill, claims bus fares when he has walked, is dishonest. But it goes further than that. A salesman who misleads a customer or makes a promise which he cannot keep is not an honest man.

Where does honesty begin and end? Everyone will defend his departure from the strict path of honesty with, to his mind, an adequate excuse.

The man who refuses to compromise his honesty in any way is sincere. You must be your own judge.

Loyalty

Shakespeare puts these words into the mouth of King Richard II:

> "The purest treasure mortal times afford
> Is spotless reputation; that away,
> Men are but gilded loam or painted clay,
> A jewel in a ten-times-barr'd-up chest
> Is a bold spirit in a loyal breast.
> Mine honour is my life; both grow in one;
> Take honour from me, and my life is done."

To have "a bold spirit in a loyal breast"—isn't that what we would all want? Bold enough to be loyal in face of difficulties, or when we feel that we have been wronged by customers, employers, or friends.

The test of loyalty does not come when your affairs are prospering and when your contribution is being praised; it comes when you are out of favour, and your efforts are being frowned upon.

Many salesmen, with customers who have complaints, blame a works manager or sales manager for what has gone wrong. This is disloyal. Other salesmen speak harshly of their companies and belittle the efforts of the management. Some criticise their company's product to customers. They would still call themselves loyal.

If a salesman cannot be loyal to his firm, he should leave it. If a sales manager cannot be loyal to his salesmen, he should be dismissed.

It is not disloyalty to leave a company for better terms and conditions elsewhere. Loyalty does not bind you to one company for ever. But so long as you are employed by a company, you must give it your whole loyalty. No one can be sincere and disloyal at the same time.

Be a good listener

Most of us talk too much. We think our own conversation so interesting, and we know the other fellow's by heart.

7

Unfortunately, the other man feels just the same way about us. Doctor Johnson said, "*The misfortune of Goldsmith is that he goes on without knowing how to get off.*" Does this happen to you? Do you ever go from one subject to another without knowing when to stop?

Martial said: "*What a long time you take to say nothing.*"

Many years ago I called on a prospect at her boutique to sell her a unit heater. She was a charming woman, who listened patiently while I explained the intricacies of the installation work and the beautiful finish of the case. I told her, as well, of the wonders of our factory and the speed of our service. But I didn't get the order. Later I noticed that a rival heater had been installed, and I asked her for the reason. She answered simply: "You didn't tell me if your heater would keep me warm."

I had talked so much and forgotten the one point that mattered.

Will Rogers said: "*A good listener is not only popular everywhere, but after a while he knows something.*" When you listen to your customers instead of talking all the time, you often learn a great deal.

What kind of talker are you? Do you know that you may talk too much? If you don't realise this, you will become an incurable talker.

Are you a pouncer? In other words, you rarely allow anyone to complete a story. You may be with a friend who is telling you his holiday experiences. He begins: "I went to the travel agency to book for . . ." Without letting him finish you interrupt to tell him: "You should have gone to Boon's. They are the best agents I know. When we went to Italy last year . . ."

Maybe a friend has had his chimney catch fire. He says to you: "Last evening our chimney caught fire. You ought to have seen the mess . . ." So you jump in with: "I bet the fire brigade were late. When the same thing happened to me I don't know how it would have ended if I had gone on waiting.

First of all, I used some salt. Did you try that? Well, I rang the brigade..."

Then there is the health pouncer. You say to a friend: "How are you?" He starts to reply: "Not too well I'm afraid, I have got..." But you interrupt with: "Do you know when I got up this morning the pain in my back was so bad I just don't know how I carried on..."

Perhaps you have decided that you are not a pouncer. If so, are you a pouncer-capper? He not only interrupts, but caps every story. Suppose someone says: "We went out last evening and had a delightful three-course meal..." Before he can tell you where he had the meal or what he ate, you are eagerly telling him: "You should try Blotto's one day. They serve a six-course dinner with wine, and all the film stars go there. The other day I saw..."

Don't be a pouncer, and don't be a pouncer-capper. Sincere men are good listeners; they are sincerely interested in other people.

Wandering eyes

A rabid talker can be turned into a good listener. If you are in the first category, force yourself to keep silent when someone else is talking. Never interrupt. Never by gesture or expression indicate that you are bursting to say your piece. Look as if you are listening. Don't let your eyes wander round the room. Nothing is more annoying than to know that a listener is only pretending to listen. You may be telling someone in a hotel lounge what is, to you, a most interesting story. Suddenly you realise that he is not listening, but following the movements of everyone passing through the swing doors. He is not even paying you the compliment of pretending to be interested in your story.

Develop the habit of being an *intent* listener.

Four into one

For a selling personality you must combine four personalities. Here they are again:

A cheerful personality;
A strong personality;
A friendly personality;
A sincere personality.

This chapter has had two aims. The first is to clarify the selling personality, and the second to convince you that one of a salesman's greatest assets is a knowledge of human relations. Each personality is based on the maxim: *Let us do unto others as we would have others do unto us.*

Can one live up to that precept? I doubt it. Only a saint could follow all the advice in this chapter. But we can aim for perfection, although we may fall short. Perhaps we cannot smile all the time. There is a time when we lose our temper. We cannot constantly listen, listen, listen, or always refrain from criticism, but we must constantly try, try, and try again to accomplish them. We must make the effort to give praise where it is due, to refuse to flatter, to eschew bluntness. This is a daily battle we must all fight and win.

When we succeed, we mould ourselves into better salesmen, and more important, into better men.

CHAPTER VII

THE GREATEST LESSON IN SELLING

When I was 22, I had been selling for five-and-a-half years. I started as a salesman, in my 17th year, because there were queues then for a vacancy as an underpaid office-boy. Tired of joining them, I took the advice of a relative who was a highly successful salesman and made my first attempt to emulate him.

I persuaded the secretary of an association uniting tobacconists against price-cutting to employ me. My job was to obtain more members. The association did not last long and it was not helped by my inability to recruit tobacconists into it. After that, I had a series of jobs selling to retailers, wholesalers, and direct to users.

I had not been outstandingly successful when, once more dissatisfied, I heard of a job which seemed worth while. A Frenchman named Simon had successfully imported silk materials from Lyons, in France. He sold to leading stores and to clothes manufacturers. The company I was with had offices next to those of Simon and his associates. When I heard that Simon wanted an assistant, I made haste to call on him. I told him: "I would very much like to join you. I have nearly six years of good sales experience, and I am looking for an opportunity of helping to build a big business."

Simon seemed to be interested in me and suggested that, before either of us made a decision, we should spend a day together. I readily agreed.

The following Tuesday morning I met Simon at nine outside John Lewis, the well-known store in Oxford Street, London. Our first call brought a big order. Simon was warmly welcomed everywhere. He had charm and a strong personality. All day I listened and admired.

At five we had tea in a Lyons Tea Shop, and I was anxious to learn whether Simon would take me on. As I had said very little during the day, I wondered how he could judge me. He talked of Paris, the manufacture of silks, of store buyers and politics, but not about me. At last I could stand it no longer and burst out with: "Mr. Simon, I really enjoyed today and know that I can help you. Will you employ me?"

"Well," he answered, "you have found out more about me, but I don't know very much about you. Tell me what you have been doing."

I told him. I explained how I had started with the tobacconist association, which had to fail as it competed with another old-established association. Then I went on to tell him that I had left the A company because they were very old-fashioned and their prices were not competitive; that the B company had not taken my advice to spend more money on advertising, and, without advertising, consumer products could not be sold; that the C company had a most difficult sales manager and no one could work with him; that the D company, selling mechanical equipment, did not have an adequate service staff to back up the sales I made. So I catalogued my failures, which, up to that moment I had thought of as my successes.

As I finished Simon said: "And so, Mr. Tack, you have always been right and everyone else wrong." At that moment, for the first time in my life, I saw myself as others saw me. The fight left me, and I remember saying, in great humility: "What, then, is wrong with me, Mr. Simon?"

His answer was quite short: "You are a bad salesman, that's all."

"But," I began, "I have experience and I have been selling or nearly six years. . . ." He stopped me and said: "Experience does not necessarily teach anyone anything. If you had been a good salesman, you would surely have succeeded with one of the companies you have mentioned. Your excuses are used by all salesmen who fail. They blame lack of success on some shortcomings of their employers."

"How, then," I pleaded, "can I become a first-class sales-man?"

"I cannot give you the answer to that," he replied. "But most salesmen, both young and old, would improve if they *stopped* selling."

He was not telling me to get an easier job, but to make a deeper study of the relationship between buyer and salesman. Many salesmen have proudly announced that they have been paid a handsome compliment by a customer.

"Do you know what he said?" they will exclaim, "He told me I was the best salesman who had called on him that week."

Only a bad salesman believes that the customer is compli-menting him on his salesmanship. He would be better advised to worry about criticism directed at him. For he made it obvious to the customer that he was making an effort to take an order, and this is the worst form of salesmanship.

Selling has been called *the gentle art of giving other people your own way*. That sums it up pretty well. You know that high pressure selling isn't selling at all and that an aggressive salesman will soon find himself on the pavement. Nevertheless a salesman must be determined to obtain an order. But the determination mustn't show.

When Simon told me to stop selling, he didn't necessarily mean that I had been too aggressive or too forceful. He meant that I was being too much of a salesman. I wasn't being my natural self. My manner and mannerisms, my voice and expressions, many of the words I used were not found in my normal conversation. What applied to me then applies to many salesmen now. They act like salesmen, they sound like salesmen. They may have the servility of the weak man or the dynamism of a regular quota-buster, but they are frightening the customer. Even top men could improve if they sharpened their selling techniques.

What makes a buyer nervous of a salesman? When he knows that an attempt is being made to make him take a line of action. Now the attempt is made at every sale. But a first-class salesman doesn't betray this purpose to the buyer, whether he be managing director, store buyer, works manager, or the owner of a small retail shop. Each buyer likes to feel that he is making his own decision without being swayed by the salesman's arguments. But he *is* swayed by the good salesman, who will always outsell the poor salesman even when the latter has a price advantage. That is what Simon was trying to tell me.

Market research

After Simon had explained the reasons for my failure as a salesman, I returned home a very perplexed young man. During the following days, weeks, and months, my brother, who was selling engineering equipment, and I, discussed methods of *stopping selling* that would result in more orders.

After a while we came to this conclusion: Whenever we were selling to customers who knew us well, and from whom we invariably had orders, we sold to them in a conversational manner as if they were friends or relatives. There was no need for any act. From that we concluded that the secret of successful selling was the adoption of a conversational sales presentation. This was the beginning of *conversational selling*, since recognised as the finest form of salesmanship. It is *the gentle art of giving other people your own way.*

Having made this important decision, we tried to prove its validity by selling to everyone as if they were friends. When one friend tries to convince another that they should holiday abroad instead of touring the Lake District, he is usually selling in a highly professional way. But neither he nor his friend realises he is selling at all. Conversational selling is simply the most effective way for one person to influence the mind of another. Then we made call after call on difficult customers, but were disappointed that for all our conversational salesmanship, they stayed as difficult as ever. It was quite disheartening, for we had felt so close to a solution to our problem.

We sought again, to find the reason for the success of conversational selling with buyers who bought from us rather than having to be sold, while it failed when the objections came thick and fast. At last we understood that conversational selling relaxed ourselves and the buyer. We did not talk naturally to a prickly customer, because we were too tense. Our tensions were transferred to the customer. That was the major factor. We lost sales because the buyer was tense. Our conclusion, which has proved itself correct in all circumstances, was that *a tense buyer never buys*. We had to find a way to relax in order to sell conversationally to difficult buyers. This would relax them, and selling would be much easier. Many buyers are difficult because they are afraid that the salesman will push his goods. Tensions are caused by a salesman who drives hard for one order and whose forcefulness is apparent to the buyer.

A salesman of such consumer goods as groceries, or confectionery, who has been with the same company for twenty years, might think that this could not happen to him as he knows all his buyers so well. Many may be his friends and they are never tense when he calls. This man is deceiving himself. He is not a salesman, but an order-taker who fills in a form at each visit and does not fight hard to introduce a new line or one that is more profitable to his company, or to increase the size of his order.

There are many order-takers in the consumer-goods field. They consistently sell well because of their company's advertising, but they would increase sales if they tried to sell when the customer says "no".

If the customer doesn't say *no*, no selling is necessary. The order-taker can change his ways, but he must watch out for tension. After taking his usual order, he might say: "Mr. Jones, you will want to stock up heavily on our new line of detergents. This is a complete breakaway from the usual products, and you will benefit in many ways from stocking now because. . . ."

A doctor examining the customer at this moment would diagnose that tensions were being aroused. He may stock all the leading brands and not want any more. As the order-taker refuses to give in and continues to sell, the more tense becomes the customer. For the first time he will want to see the back of his so-called friend, so he will make excuses like:

"Leave it for the time being until I have taken stock."

"I have just had a big delivery of brand XYZ."

"I have another appointment now but I will see you next time."

When a speciality salesman calls for the first time on a prospect and begins his sales presentation, tensions set in straight away. Every good speciality salesman knows that he must first relax a prospect.

It isn't easy to buy. Buyers who place orders as a daily routine do not easily brush off a salesman. Even kindly men may be brusque to the point of rudeness. Others make promises they have no intention of keeping. This may seem absurd, but buyers have the same reactions as salesmen, and, as we have said, are often intimidated by those men who sell too strongly. The salesman who cannot get a second appointment with a buyer can blame his bad selling tactics on the first call.

Remember that we are all buyers at some time or another. We are often reluctant to leave a shop without buying something. It seems so easy and straightforward to tell a shop assistant that he has nothing to suit us and that we will look elsewhere. But we rarely do it. We make up excuses instead. We pretend that we must match colours, or consult another member of the family, and even say that we will call back in a short while to make the purchase, when we have no intention of doing so. For when an assistant is persuading us to buy and we object, tensions set in. If the assistant did not sell so forcefully and knew how to relax us, he might get the sale in spite of our doubts.

When we learned that a tense customer doesn't buy, we knew we had to relax him. Conversational selling can do this, but only if it comes naturally. If it is forced, we are still giving the salesman's standard jargon, and it is obvious. Thus it was clear that we could sell conversationally only when we were relaxed and that it was impossible to sell conversationally when we were tense. The solution to the problem was to remove our own tensions when selling.

Learning to relax

When we decided that the art of selling was to relax the buyer—that conversational selling relaxed the buyer, and that it was only possible to sell conversationally when relaxed—we studied various methods of relaxation.

But the advice given in books and by so-called authorities was contradictory. One book said it was essential to relax for at least forty minutes every day. We tried and gave up. We could not understand our failure then, but now we know that beginners cannot relax for long. No one can sleep every afternoon for thirty minutes or so, and even reading a book for half-an-hour is not truly relaxing. Many people stay tense even when asleep, and wake up tired and with a sense of strain. To stay awake but utterly relaxed for thirty minutes is impossible for most of us.

Another expert recommended a sloping plank for relaxing upon; one must stretch out on it every day with the head lower than the feet. When we tried this, manipulating the plank brought on tension.

Most people get tense as they prepare for relaxation. It seemed to us that the power of mind, especially the worried mind, was not taken into account. To advise an anxious man that he must make his mind a blank for even ten minutes is to ask the impossible. It is as if a non-swimmer were told that he must plough his way through at least a mile of water in order to swim. It was this analogy that decided us that, just as a non-swimmer might cover two or three yards before giving up and then be encouraged to increase the distance gradually, one could learn to relax completely for a few seconds to begin with and then increase the period to five minutes.

The more we investigated the more we found that very few understood the meaning of relaxation. The physician who advises a patient to relax more, is often so tense himself that he takes barbiturates to calm himself at the end of a day. His advice to the over-tense patient is to find a hobby, go for a holiday, or take up some sport. He forgets that a hobby or sport provides only temporary relief from tensions. I have been addicted to most sports in the past, and now look forward to week-end golf. Golf is great exercise, especially for the middle-aged, but when I look around the clubhouse at the end of a morning I cannot say that everyone there is quite relaxed. Many are overwrought at the way they have played.

Learning to relax takes time but little effort. Many students at our courses believed they were completely relaxed until they were shown that, in some circumstances, they could become very tense. One student might be asked: "Would you enjoy reciting to the audience a simple nursery rhyme, like 'Mary had a little lamb?'" He will hesitate a moment, and then mumble that he would do it but without any enjoyment in the performance. Another might be asked if he would feel happy going on to the platform to recite "Mary had a little lamb." He usually pales at the thought. The whole class is then asked if anyone would feel happy speaking the same rhyme at the Albert Hall before 5,000 people and television cameras. No one would. If the Albert Hall experiment were tried, the student, unless he was an experienced public speaker, would develop a somersaulting stomach, perspire freely, and would not remember whether Mary was leading a little lamb or driving a Rolls-Royce.

Tension does that to those who undertake some task that is unnatural to them. Even though most salesmen attending our courses are very experienced, they get highly nervous and tense if asked to speak in public. The reason is that they are not orators, and so inexperienced in speaking from a platform. Should a student be a practised public speaker, he would not mind. A doctor explains it like this:

"On being asked to come to the platform to recite, the student's muscles tense. Fear messages rush to the brain and the brain returns these messages to the muscles, which become even more tense. Tense muscles form poisons, which travel through the bloodstream. These cloud the mind, and the thoughts become still more muddled. More messages to the muscles—more tension, more muddle, and so on."

Selling is unnatural to most salesmen. It is far more natural to give up than to persuade someone to change his mind. If a customer has decided to buy, no selling is necessary. Selling influences the wavering mind, and most people do not like to be influenced in this way. The salesman instinctively knows that and that is why he is tense when:

1. He begins his career in selling. He may pass customer after customer before facing one.
2. He calls upon a difficult buyer and much depends on his call.

Some salesmen are tense at every call, others when they must sell hard, and these tensions undermine a man's work in the field.

Any salesman who learns to relax will not only become a better salesman but will lead a happier life.

Enthusiasm and relaxation

Many sales executives, hearing that we teach relaxation, become concerned that their inexperienced salesmen will become too relaxed and adopt a "couldn't-care-less" attitude to the customer. But the relaxed person does not have this sloppy attitude. It belongs to the *poseur*, the man without confidence, who lounges and droops around a shop or office displaying lack of enthusiasm and determination.

The relaxed salesman can be enthusiastic and inspiring in his sales talk. His mind is clear, and so can deal with any objection. Because he feels better, he looks alert and keen. He can also work hard without suffering the stresses and strains of modern business life. Surely every managing director would like to employ such a salesman.

Relaxing step by step

It takes a long time to learn to relax. There is no short cut. Most salesmen, while appreciating the need to relax, give up after two or three weeks because they see no benefit in it. Benefit cannot be derived from relaxation exercises until they become a habit and this can take from four to six months. Just as we all take up some hobby with tremendous enthusiasm that dies away after a short while, so the salesman learning to relax often gives up too quickly.

To learn to sell conversationally, you must follow a few simple exercises day after day, week after week, month after month. That is the way to achieve relaxation. When that time comes and you are in a situation that would normally tense your muscles, you will automatically relax. We found the easy way to relax when we learned that it was impossible to do so for thirty minutes or more at a time. We could relax parts of the body for a minute or so without any trouble. For a minute, the brain can concentrate and the mind will not wander.

HOW TO TRAIN YOURSELF TO RELAX

Relaxing must become a habit. You give so little time to it that it doesn't become a strain. It doesn't worry you, and set up negative thoughts.

Most people can concentrate for a minute at a time.

If I ask you to think of your hand for a few seconds, you

can do so. The first step then is to divide the body into seven parts.

They are:

Your left-arm muscles
Your right-arm muscles
Your left-leg muscles
Your right-leg muscles
Your stomach and chest muscles
Your back muscles
Your face muscles

Think for a moment of your left arm. That's easy enough, isn't it? You must think about it for just a minute later on. Before concentrating on your muscles, however, you must remember two words. They are not especially original, for they have been used by teachers of relaxation for many years. If you tell yourself to relax it doesn't have much effect. But if you tell a muscle, or a part of your body, to "let go," then after a while, it does just that—it lets itself go. To anybody who is tense, we say: "For goodness sake, let yourself go!"

So far you must remember only seven parts of your body and the two words, "let go".

Now begin the minute technique. Start tonight when you go to bed. Lie flat on your back and for only one minute— and it doesn't matter if it is a little less—concentrate all your thoughts on the muscles of your left arm. Don't worry about the rest of your body, merely the left arm. Now tense the muscles as much as you can. Then tell them to "let go". Say the word "let" as you breathe in, "go" as you breathe out. Do that for one minute, and then put it out of your mind.

Next day, when you have a little spare time (perhaps after lunch or while you are waiting to see someone), concentrate on that left arm again, and once more tell the muscles to let go. Continue like this for seven days. You will know when the muscles are properly relaxed, because you will get a warm, tingling feeling in them—and it is a very comfortable feeling.

Few people can relax even an arm muscle without practice. You can prove it to yourself by asking a friend to relax and then lifting his left arm high into the air. You will rarely find that it will drop when you let it go. He will either hold it in the air or bring it down slowly. He is not at all relaxed because, if he were, the left arm would fall to his side automatically.

The second week

During the second week you must concentrate all your thoughts on your right arm. Think about it for one minute, two or three times a day and when you go to bed. Forget all about your left arm. You will find that it will automatically relax itself, but don't worry about it.

The third week

During the third week you will carry out the same procedure with your left leg.

For this you must be sitting down, or lying in bed. When sitting, don't cross your legs but put your feet flat on the ground.

The fourth week

For the fourth week, concentrate on your right leg muscles ignoring your arms and your left leg.

The fifth week

The fifth week is given over to your stomach and chest muscles. Once again, don't forget to tense your muscles first, and then let go.

The sixth week

The sixth week is the turn of your back muscles.

The seventh week

Your facial muscles take up the seventh week. Your teeth

must not be clenched. There must be no wrinkles on your forehead.

Now a warning. Don't hurry! Remember this is a long-term exercise. Spend two weeks on each part of your body rather than cut the time down.

Assuming good progress, you will relax completely in seven weeks. For the following two or three months, concentrate your thoughts on your entire body, and let all your muscles go. Remember, for a minute only at a time. Then you will find, as many others have already, that you will relax automatically. And that was your initial aim.

Only after six months have passed should you try to relax for longer than a minute at a time.

How does this technique differ from others? It makes relaxing an unconscious habit. It will happen to you if you follow these instructions for six to nine months.

Make the effort. Don't expect miracles the first week or so. You will not detect much difference for quite a while. Then it happens quickly. Here are the rules again:

1. Remember these seven parts of the body:
     the left arm muscles
     the right arm muscles
     the left leg muscles
     the right leg muscles
     the stomach and chest muscles
     the back muscles
     the face muscles

2. Remember to lie flat on your back, and the words "let go."

3. Start with the left arm. Tense it. Tell the muscles to "let go" and repeat this for one minute. Start tonight when you go to bed. Then repeat it two or three times a day.

4. Concentrate on your left arm alone for the first seven to ten days.

8

5. After this, concentrate on your right arm and forget your left arm. Carry on for seven to ten days.

6. Concentrate in turn on the remaining five parts of your body allotting seven to ten days for each part.

7. After two or three months, carry out the same "let go" procedure with your whole body.

8. After six months practise relaxation regularly, but increase the time to from two to five minutes for each period.

9. You must maintain the short daily relaxing exercises until your muscles respond automatically at the least sign of tension.

Now for some don'ts:

Don't tense your muscles more than once in each session. You tense them only in order to sense the difference between relaxation and tension.

Don't try to relax your whole body while sitting down. Rest your arms on your uncrossed legs, and concentrate on relaxing your arms and legs only.

Don't wrinkle your forehead, or close your eyelids, or your mouth tightly, when relaxing your facial muscles.

That is all you must know to make relaxing a habit.

Our system has been successful because it is easy to master. The art of good salesmanship is to sell in a conversational manner, and, when you train yourself to relax, you will begin to sell naturally and more efficiently.

CHAPTER VIII

THE SALES PRESENTATION

The scene is set in Capulet's Orchard.

Enter Romeo.

ROMEO: He jests at scars that never felt a wound.
> (Juliet appears above at a window.)
> But soft! What light through yonder window breaks?
> It is the east, and Juliet is the sun!
> Arise, fair sun, and kill the envious moon
> Who is already sick and pale with grief
> That thou her maid art far more fair than she:
> Be not her maid, since she is envious;

What would happen if an actor decided to alter Shakespeare's words, if he decided to cut out a line here and add a line there? It doesn't happen, because Shakespeare achieved as near perfection as possible.

From his perfection there is a lesson applicable to all salesmen. It is: *Don't tamper with that which is right.*

If you knew the one ideal word sequence that would bring orders from every customer, you would use it at every call, wouldn't you? This perfection is unobtainable, but all salesmen should aim to present their proposition to every customer in the best possible manner.

Studying the buyer

It is hard to judge a buyer by his appearance or mannerisms. How, then, can we find the best way to sell to every type of buyer, a man or a woman, a store buyer or a works manager, a managing director or an office manager, a farmer or a builder? Does psychology help? Not very much. The type of man who reads most books on psychology should keep as far away from this subject as possible. A business transaction must be based on something more specific. I have not heard of a psychologist being a first-class salesman.

We can learn from industrial psychology, but only when it is allied to comprehensible facts. Although buyers vary in shapes and sizes, moods and customs, they all buy for the same basic reason: it benefits them or their company to do so. Each product or service has many benefits, these will be analysed later. You will be shown how to discover the main benefit of your merchandise or service. To sell perfectly on every occasion, you must discover the best means of explaining benefits to a buyer.

Some salesmen consider themselves so well-versed in psychology, and believe they understand each customer so well that they can read his mind and tell him everything he wants to hear. This is sheer nonsense, but too many salesmen deceive themselves into believing they are mind-readers.

As far back as 1934, J. B. Rhine, of Duke University, delved deeply into parapsychology. Many tests were carried out. The simplest involved using a pack of cards. One person chose a card and concentrated on it, while a second person elsewhere attempted to read his mind and guess the card. Obviously, the tests were much more involved than this explanation suggests, but they all came under severe criticism. It was generally agreed that there was no proof that one person could read the mind of another. There are, of course, many recorded instances of telepathic coincidences. Someone, perhaps, has a sudden feeling that a relative is ill, and later discovers that at that very moment the relative did, in fact, have an accident. But is this telepathy, or coincidence? No one has yet given an adequate answer. If, therefore, the researchers into parapsychology cannot prove that one person can read another's mind, even when two people are in sympathy with one another, how can anyone claim that he can read the mind of a buyer?

Mind-reading, however, is what some salesmen call a

predictable reaction to a selling technique. But this is not mind-reading; it is salesmanship. We know that a buyer is interested only in benefits. Suppose that a product has eight main benefits, which we shall call a, b, c, d, e, f, g, and h. The mind-reader might estimate that the main interests of a buyer would be centred on points a, b, f, and g. He could be lucky and be right, but he could also be very wrong. Maybe the buyer's main interests were in a, b, d, and e. The mind-reader would have missed out two important selling points. Wouldn't he have been wiser to explain every benefit from a to h? In that way he could dispense with mind-reading or psychology; he would know that he had given the buyer every benefit, and taken every opportunity to complete an order.

Friendship

Although it has been stressed that human relations, coupled with a selling personality, contribute to an order, it will not alone suffice if hard selling is necessary. Many salesmen make good friends of their customers, but a buyer rarely places an order solely because of his friendly relationship with a salesman. He will only do this if the 'friend' offers competitive products. The man who has won goodwill after many years of excellent service always has an advantage over a competitor.

The 'order-taker' selling consumer goods will keep his customers by friendship so long as he has goods they want. If he changed his job and sold less competitive products, he would find that the customer, through personal regard, might give him some small orders, but the large orders would go elsewhere.

Friendship enables the salesman to obtain a good hearing. After that, it is his ability that counts. Friendship will not sway the group buyer of a chain store to place an order, but it will get a salesman a quick hearing from that buyer. He need only telephone for an immediate appointment, while another man could kick his heels in a waiting room for a long time before being seen. Many salesmen believe they are regarded highly by customers, when the reverse is true; this also applies the other way round.

Many buyers think they are liked and respected by all who call on them. Recently a buyer told me that salesmen always received fair treatment, and so they would always bring him special lines. But that buyer is wrong. He is not too popular with salesmen. He breaks appointments; he is curt; he keeps them waiting unnecessarily; he is full of his own importance. Just as that buyer is mistaken, so are many salesmen who believe that a buyer is a true friend when he has a low opinion of them. You can test this for yourself. How often have you left a customer with feelings almost of hatred welling up within you? But your manner might still persuade the customer that you have a high regard for him.

When we carried out research amongst buyers to test their likes and dislikes, we proved that salesmen cannot rely on friendship alone to obtain orders. We invited a panel of buyers, including shop owners, garage proprietors, managing directors, store buyers and works managers, to complete a questionnaire on buyer-salesman relationship. One of the questions asked was: *What percentage of salesmen who have called on you for five years or more do you*

like very much?
like?
tolerate?
dislike?
dislike very much?

Only 6% came in the first group. Where would you be? Wouldn't it be wiser to assume that you are only tolerated? Then you would always depend on your selling personality *and* sales ability to obtain orders.

Experienced salesmen do not accept this. They refuse to see themselves as others see them and that is why they often remain as salesmen and get embittered because they do not achieve promotion.

In book publishing, particularly, friendship between sales-man and buyer is highly rated. All the 'old hands' believe that, as they have been on the road so long and know their buyers well, they have only to show their lists to take orders. Many years ago, when Boots had libraries in each shop, I spoke about this to their book buyer. I said: "You must be a very busy man. There are so many publishers with so many salesmen, and each must see you regularly with his new books. You must hold the record for seeing the highest num-ber of salesmen each day. How many do you actually see?"

He smiled and answered: "Perhaps one a day. Sometimes I go days without seeing one."

I looked as astonished as I felt. "But", I said, "this is im-possible...."

"No, it isn't," he interrupted. "You used the word 'sales-men'. I see dozens of representatives each week, but very, very few salesmen." Later he told me of the small regard he had for those who called upon him regularly but were never enthusiastic about a book, never really sold him on the idea that a book was going to be a good seller. All they seemed to know about most books were the titles.

Many times since I have heard publishers' representatives excuse their lack of success by claiming that book-selling was the hardest form of salesmanship. The truth is that they don't sell. Some of the best publishers' representatives I know are men who do not live in the past but learn modern salesman-ship techniques. A good salesman does not rely on friendship any more than on mind-reading. He depends on the *words* he uses.

Words

There are many aids to person-to-person selling. Sales brochures, demonstration models, samples, filmstrips, photo-graphs, and drawings all play their part. Just imagine what would happen if a company produced the most elaborate and expensive sales brochure in the history of marketing. Many designers were used for it. Eminent artists were brought in to help. Typographers spent hours deciding the type face. Paper manufacturers made special paper for this important and grand publication.

At last it is out, and a copy is sent to a salesman. He approaches a customer and, lips tight shut he produces the brochure. He indicates various drawings and pages of print, says nothing. He relies entirely on the brochure to sell his goods for him. Would he take an order? Certainly not. The customer would not read all the printed matter and, although perhaps interested in the beautiful layout and photographs and full of admiration for the designer, he would not make a decision on such incomplete evidence. He would need explanations. He would raise objections and would want answers. If this were not so, every company would merely produce a brochure, post it to a buyer, and expect an order by return of post.

While such a sales aid might help a salesman, it can do no more. If a salesman does not speak, he cannot sell. If it were possible to market without person-to-person selling, a company would sell by direct mail. A salesman is paid to sell and that means to talk. He may make a living without using a single sales aid, but a sales aid alone cannot earn a living for a salesman who doesn't make use of the right words at the right time. *A salesman, therefore, lives by the words he uses.*

You must agree with that. You will also agree that if you knew that certain words had sales appeal while others did not register, you would use only words that brought positive results. You might find these words were not helping your sale along:

I wonder. . . .
I think. . . .
I hope. . . .
It possibly. . . .

In their place you could use—

I am sure. . . .
I know. . . .
I am certain. . . .
It will. . . .

You would use these words because you have confidence in your goods. If you haven't, you shouldn't be selling them. A salesman succeeds because he chooses the right words and bans all negative words. But he doesn't use words in isolation. They are strung together in sentences. *Therefore, better sentences mean better selling.*

It would be unusual if a sale resulted from the use of one or two sentences only. Sentences are linked to form a sales story, or sales presentation, or sales sequence. *Therefore, a better sales story must mean better selling.*

What we have arrived at logically, all *good* salesmen prove from their experience. Every salesman uses some form of sales sequence and on its strength depends his results. If any salesman tape-recorded a series of his interviews with customers, he would find a basic theme running through them. Certain sentences would be constantly used:

This line is selling very well.
It will pay for itself over and over again.
You will have sole rights for this area.
It will help you to make extra customers.
Our advertising campaign will be the biggest. . . .
Just look at this new advertisement. . . .
We are launching a new T.V. advertising campaign.

If these sentences are not part of a sales sequence, what are they? Unfortunately, they are weakened because they are so commonly used. Competitive salesmen might use exactly the same sentences. The average salesman has a sequence of sorts, but it is only when he perfects it that his selling is efficient.

The argument proves that you live by the words you use—that better words mean better selling, that better sentences mean better selling, and that a better sales story means much better selling.

The sales story

Most sales presentations are worked out by the salesmen themselves, as few companies take the trouble to give them sales training. When a company gives thorough training, it provides a sales story as its basis. A salesman's own story might be good, bad or indifferent according to his ability. When a company works out a sales story, based on the experience of its leading salesmen, it can transform an average salesman into a first-class one.

A sales story is founded on the firm premise that no reputable speaker would make an important speech without writing it out many times, memorising much of it, and rehearsing it again and again. Is the salesman so different from the public speaker? The latter may motivate many, but the salesman influences the mind of just one person at a time.

The sales story can compensate for weaknesses in a salesman and give strength to the presentation of the experienced representative. It ensures that every fact is given logically at every call. It saves time, for the salesman can keep to the point without being sidetracked.

Most salesmen are interrupted. The buyer may have an unexpected caller, or a telephone call. The salesman without a story may be put off by these interruptions, but the man who has mastered a sequence merely restates briefly the main points he has covered and then continues with his planned sequence. This gives him confidence.

Why, then, do so many salesmen and sales executives dislike the idea of a sales sequence? They often misunderstand it, and are not aware of the changes that have taken place since the sales story was originated. Word-for-word presentation failed only because the rules were too rigid and too many sales executives tried to write a sales story from the office chair. This made salesmen feel that they were being turned into walking parrots. They could not sell enthusiastically if they were worried about getting the words right. But the weakness of some sales executives, and the closed minds of too many salesmen, do not destroy the fact that there is no substitute for a good sales sequence.

Our first venture into a sales sequence was the monologue patter. Although we were not happy with it, it certainly helped men to sell more effectively. The major problem was to teach the salesmen to memorise page after page of sales story, using many words and sentences which they could not speak naturally. Although showmanship is a part of salesmanship, a salesman is not an actor easily able to memorise his lines.

The selling-sentence sequence

Trial and error led us to the selling-sentence sequence. We knew it was right for a salesman to tell the best possible story at every call. We knew it was wrong for the salesman to memorise a lengthy presentation. The ideal was to tell a complete sales story in the salesman's own words but built around all the benefits of a product. So we broke the sequence down into stages, and then wrote a heading for each stage. The theory was that the salesman could memorise the headings and, armed with a few brief facts, could then elaborate each step. This did not work in practice, because the salesman could not speak in headlines and so found it difficult to remember them.

The next development was to change a headline into a sentence. Instead of the cue being a headline, the cue became a sentence, one that any salesman could remember and speak quite easily, one that would clearly indicate the ground to be covered.

And the salesman found it simple to memorise a sentence. It works like this: Our industrial group sells a wide range of heating, ventilating, and air-purifying units. When we taught the monologue sequence, one of the steps that salesmen had to memorise was:

> "It has been proved that work falls off during the afternoon. This applies in shop, office and factory, and the reason is often a heavy atmosphere. But it needn't happen to your staff. You can turn an eight-hour day into an eight-hour working day. Good ventilation will do just that for you. Opening a window would not solve your problem; it would only cause draughts and complaints from members of the staff. Some want the window open, some want it closed. And on foggy days you don't want polluted air to come in.
>
> "You will find that, with adequate ventilation there is such a changed atmosphere that you get better results from your staff. I feel sure that you yourself don't like going into your main office when several members of your staff have colds. Ventilation won't cure colds, but it does cut down the risk of cross infection. . . . "

That was just one step, in itself quite a lot to memorise. In the headline sequence it was summarised as "*better health through better ventilation*". The heading was difficult to remember. It didn't closely define the step, which stresses the profitability of staff working in a good atmosphere. When we realised the value of a selling sequence in place of a headline, we studied the step carefully to find the right sentence, and there it was, staring us in the face.

> *You can turn an eight-hour day into an*
> *eight-hour working day*

Salesmen easily remembered this sentence and that it

should be followed by an explanation of the way in which ventilation can increase output. This leading sentence could be applied to industry, or agriculture, to office, or to shop.

We went through the whole sequence and gave new salesmen sentences for each step and general guidance about elaborating them. But it was emphasised that they should use their own words and not try to follow ours rigidly. Men were no longer parrots. They need not flounder in an attempt to copy the speech of other people. The selling sequence has now stood the test of time. It is used by companies large and small throughout the world. It is taught not only to men in our own industrial divisions but to the thousands of salesmen who attend Tack courses each year, both in London and at our 17 branches overseas.

Working it all out

If a company invited the management consultancy division of our organisation to work out a selling-sentence sequence for it, this is how the consultant assigned to the job would set about it.

1. He would visit the factory where the product was manufactured. He would study as many of the manufacturing processes as possible, asking questions continually of the works manager and other members of the product division. He would be looking for special manufacturing 'benefits' which would give an advantage over competitors' goods. He would list each benefit.

2. He would visit the sales office, study all sales literature, and question all sales executives. Again, he would list benefits.

3. He would work in the field with salesmen, and with field executives if appropriate. He would listen to their sales presentations, and again list benefits. He would do more than this. He would also list each factor that could be turned into a benefit.

4. Back at his office he would list all the possible benefits of the product.

5. He would then arrange the list in a logical sequence, for every salesman must give coherence to his sales talk. He must introduce himself to a customer. This is called the *Approach*. To capture the undivided attention of the customer he must quickly arouse *Interest*. Buyers are always alert to find out that companies have not fallen behind technically. However large a company might be, it could be unknown to a buyer and the next step must be for a salesman to create *Confidence*. Then he must sell all the benefits of the *Product*. But this isn't enough. He must now *Create the Desire* to buy. Finally he must *Close* the sale.

Here are the steps that the consultant would have listed:

> The Approach.
> Creation of Interest.
> Creation of Confidence.
> Product Benefits.
> Creation of Desire.
> The Close.

6. The consultant now has the framework for his sales sequence. Based on what he has learned from working with the salesmen, he would write a sequence in full.

7. He would divide the sequence into several steps, one for the approach, another for the creation of interest, yet another for the creation of confidence. The product benefit step may need eight separate sentences, with one for each main benefit. There would be another sentence for creation of desire, and a final sentence for the close. This may total twelve sentences in all.

8. He would use the sequence himself in the field, testing it with the company's salesmen or its field executives.

9. He would then link each sentence with a sales aid, if this

were possible. He might advise the company to provide new sales aids or extra brochures to reinforce the sequence. He would aim for a visual aid for each step.

10. Then the consultant would write out each step on a separate card, along the lines of this diagram:

STEP NO. 1 THE APPROACH	EXHIBITS
SELLING SENTENCE	
POINTS TO REMEMBER	

11. The selling sentence goes on the top left-hand side of the card. In the right square is the name of the sales aid to be used at the same time. Under "Points to Remember" are three or four facts as reminders of the points he will deal with during this step.

12. The consultant would then hand the twelve cards, together with the full sequence, to a company executive. He would advise the executive to give every new recruit the twelve cards as well as a full script. The new recruit would be told not to memorise the full script, but that it might help him to build his own steps around the selling sentences. Of course, new recruits would have to memorise the twelve main sentences, but this could be done during the initial sales training.

From that moment on, the company employing our consultant would only have to alter the sentences from time to time as better ones were evolved. Some companies offer prizes to salesmen who can develop better sentences than those in current use.

This is the way that a company can teach its salesmen the selling sentences technique.

You

If you are not given a sequence by your company, you must evolve one on the lines used by our consultant. You may not be able to visit a works and question a works manager, or work with other salesmen, but you *can* intensively study your merchandise and sales literature. You will greatly enjoy working out good selling sentences, sentences with punch, sentences that help the sale along and ensure that you remember every fact and benefit.

Calling back and mixed lines

Salesmen of consumer goods do not believe that they can use a sales sequence at every call. They claim that, as they see their customers so frequently, they cannot keep to a sequence, no customer wanting to hear the same story over and over again. This is only partially true. These salesmen must open new accounts, and need strong selling. Strong selling and a sales sequence go hand-in-hand. When routine calls are made, a 'potted' sequence for special lines or promotional ideas must be devised.

There may be a new product, a new pack, a new advertising campaign or a new sales promotion tie-up. All these benefits need a simple sequence. Many salesmen of consumer goods use such weary phrases as

"We are giving away artificial flowers," or
"This is our new quick-opening pack."

These sentences have no appeal and there must be a more convincing story for a retailer to stock new products or tie-in with a promotion scheme.

If a consumer-goods salesman could eavesdrop on his fellow salesmen, he would soon learn that most of them sell in the same way, use the same sentences and sound equally lifeless.

The representative with a wide range of products can also adapt his sequence to it. For example, a man selling to the building industry may have a catalogue of 14,000 items. From this catalogue, the buyer will generally buy what he wants without having to be sold. This is the repeat business on which the 'order-taker' lives. The salesman, however, who wants to increase his sales by selling additional lines, will frame a sequence for these products. He might change his selling sentences regularly as additions are made to the range, but the effort will be well worth while. He can also often sell his products in groups.

"*Not today, thank you*"

Here is a story that has gone the rounds for the past forty years or more. It is usually told by someone who opposes a standard sales presentation. It is this:

"A salesman calls on a buyer and launches into his sequence. He begins at the approach, works slowly through each step, and half-an-hour later reaches the close. When he asks for the order, the buyer says: 'All you have succeeded in doing is wasting thirty minutes of my time. I was quite willing to buy after five minutes. I was waiting for someone like you to place an order. But you have talked so much that I've been put off buying.' "

There are several versions of this story. It could happen. It could happen to a salesman who, having no standard sales presentation, talked too much about himself and not enough about the prospect's business. But I have never known it to happen. No one has ever told me about it first-hand; it always happened to a friend of a friend of a friend.

Do not worry about wasting the time of an odd prospect or so. Tell the full story at every call. It could be wrong for one call in 200, but no one can be right all the time. The odds are always on the salesman who tells a complete story at every call.

Inconvenient

What action should a salesman take when a buyer does not seem to be in the right circumstances for placing an order?

Perhaps:

the shop is full of customers;

a buyer complains of a hangover;

a buyer has been reprimanded by one of his senior executives;

a buyer is busy stock-taking;

a buyer is in a hurry to get away.

Should the salesman launch into his sequence or should he call back at another time? No hard-and-fast rule can be laid down for these situations. No salesman would admit that he is weak. And the weak salesman too readily accepts the apparently non-selling situation.

Has the buyer a bad headache, or is he putting on an act?

Is he in a real hurry to get away?

Is he busy stock-taking, or is it an excuse?

The strong salesman will judge the truth of the situation. The weak man will raise his hat and leave. But although no rule can be laid down, if it is clear that the time and the day are wrong, a salesman should leave and return with his full story another day.

Industrial selling

Salesmen of very technical products do not believe they must sell at all. They tend to regard themselves as technicians rather than salesmen. They are ready to stress technical developments, but do not talk of the customers' interests. No sequence keeps them to the path of selling. Their lack of a plan leads them to omit main selling features. The technical salesman must have a sequence and must use it, especially when submitting a quotation.

Competitors

Should competitors' activities be included in a sales sequence? This question is often asked, but rarely applies.

The best answer to a competitor is to use the strongest possible sales sequence. Every benefit explained helps to counter the arguments of a competitive salesman. Competitors need not be mentioned, if only because a buyer will often defend a competitor's product from attack, even when he knows that the criticism is just.

If a sequence is efficient it will answer every criticism, whether from a competitor or a buyer.

If a customer raises a competitor's criticism, tell him: "He is entitled to his views. He represents a good company, but you, Mr. Brown, are interested only in what we can do for you, how you will benefit from placing your confidence in us."

It is a golden rule for all salesmen not to attack a competitor.

Demonstration

On each selling-sentence card, there is space for an exhibit or sales aid. At each step of the sale, the interest of the customer must be maintained by an appeal to one of his senses—sight, smell, touch, hearing, taste. A colourful photograph perhaps of a suite of furniture or a piece of machinery, adds to the strength of the sequence. To prove that a new kind of glue is almost odourless, let the prospect smell it for himself. When you describe the beauty of a material, let the buyer feel it. Gramophone records and tape-recorders have been used as sales aids. The salesman of a new food product may invite the buyer to taste a sample.

Sales aids must be introduced at the right time. Shown too soon a sample may merit only a casual glance. Held back too long, the buyer may have already made up his mind before it is shown. Sales aids include demonstration models, photographs, drawings, newspaper cuttings, laboratory tests, testimonial letters, reports, graphs, samples, packs, materials, and so on.

Everything, from the sample-carrying case to the largest demonstration model, is a sales aid. It must be immaculate in appearance and efficient in operation.

A salesman tried to sell us a photo-copying machine. "Here it is," he said, putting it on our desk. It could be seen at once that it was anything but new. The casing was scratched and looked as though tea had been spilt over it. We awaited the demonstration. After asking us for some literature to have copied, he put it in the machine and we expected a perfect replica. It was anything but perfect; something had gone wrong. "Damn," said the salesman. "The blasted thing has been playing me up all the week."

When salesmen ask for our advice, we often suggest that they should bring their sales kit with them. Most of their sales brochures are dog-eared, crumpled and soiled.

Here are some rules for demonstrating:

1. If your demonstration unit is not in perfect condition, refuse to have it. Ask your company to change it.
2. Do not apologise for a demonstration unit that is not working correctly because of some flaw that became apparent at a previous call. In this case, don't demonstrate at all.
3. Let the prospect sell himself by allowing him to work your model.
4. Demonstrate slowly. Make sure that your prospect is following each point.
5. Make sure that you know your demonstration model so thoroughly that if a breakdown occurs you can put it right without the prospect being aware of what has happened.
6. If your demonstration model can damage or mark furniture, take precautions against its happening at the outset.

My brother, George Tack, describes *the art of demonstration* this way:

"For many years people in London's West End streets have been entertained by an escapologist and his partner. The escape artist is tied up in chains so that he can scarcely move. The chains are then padlocked, but after a considerable struggle he frees himself in full view of the public. To watch these men at work is an object lesson in the art of building up excitement and tension in a small, sceptical crowd.

"The method adopted to gather an audience is both simple and effective. Having found a suitable site, with no policemen in the offing, their first step is to remove the chains from a sack and throw them onto the pavement with plenty of flourish and clatter. The man to be tied up then removes a portion of his clothing and spends some minutes flexing his muscles and breathing deeply.

"During this display, his partner starts the patter calculated to bring passers-by to a stop to see what is going to happen. When a reasonable crowd has collected, the tying-up process begins. This is accompanied by a series of gasps and groans from the man being chained. When he is finally padlocked and lying on the ground he appears to be both in agony, and inescapably imprisoned. By this time the crowd, having grown appreciably, is asked to close in so as not to take up too much room and allow others to see this 'remarkable performance'. Everybody then waits patiently for the escape to take place, but until the 'barker' has a large enough audience he continues talking. Only then does he whip off his cap and make his collection for his partner on the ground. But until he has collected every penny possible he keeps the crowd waiting for the escape.

"There is nothing particularly novel about this type of showmanship; it has been used ever since man first attempted to entertain his fellow men. Even today's great stage magicians use a similar technique. Analyse their performances and it will be found that in a twenty-minute show their patter will take up considerably more time than the tricks they perform.

"Here, then, we have the basic principles of good demonstration, but it is surprising how few salesmen use this technique in their daily work. Every salesman has something to demonstrate—a sample product, a working model, a new pack, blueprints, or literature which, whether in booklet or leaflet form, should be shown in the correct manner to a prospective customer.

"The secret is to use the method of the showman and hold back the demonstration as long as possible. Whet the customer's appetite and arouse his enthusiasm *before* he sees what you have to show. The longer you keep him waiting the more anxious he will be to see your demonstration. Arouse his curiosity and you will maintain his interest. Also you will be able to talk benefits more easily before the demonstration than after it.

"Even when it is only a question of showing the prospect literature, the same rule applies. Talk first, holding the booklet or pamphlet in your hand, and then show the customer what you want him to see, in the order in which you want him to see it. Never hand the literature to him to study while you stand by; you will only watch him skim over the pages without taking in anything he is reading, and you will have lost control of the sale.

"What about the salesman who has neither a model nor a sample, and whose literature is not suitable for showing customers? The man, for example, who sells ideas. He, too, is able to demonstrate with one of the most useful sales aids a salesman carries—pencil and paper! The method is simple enough; as early as possible in the sale produce a notebook and write down some of the points you wish to make. Try to obtain the prospect's agreement to each of them. You will be using figures, or prices, or special terms, or even drawing rough sketches; whichever you write down will arouse and maintain his attention.

"A good demonstration is the best way of selling *anything* and, assisted by a well-prepared sequence you can transform demonstrations into SALES."

To train yourself to sell successfully, develop the perfect sales sequence. Evolve strong selling sentences and dramatise your story by the use of effective sales aids.

CHAPTER IX

THE PRE-APPROACH

Here are some scenes of a salesman in action:

Scene I. A Works Manager's Office

WORKS MANAGER: The idea seems good, but it won't be easy to incorporate it in our system. Have you a drawing?

SALESMAN [*delving into his bag*]: Yes, of course, here it is. No, it isn't. Ah, this is the one [*taking out a crumpled piece of paper*]. Sorry, that's a drawing of the larger unit. [*He rummages again, muttering*] Where is the confounded thing? I know it's here somewhere; I was using it only an hour ago. This should be it. . . .

Couldn't happen? Doesn't happen? It occurs over and over again.

In the pre-approach, every sample, every sales aid, every brochure, must be packed so neatly that a salesman can extract any piece he requires without taking his eyes away from the customer.

Scene II. A Receptionist's Office

RECEPTIONIST: May I help you?

SALESMAN: I want to see the man who buys.

RECEPTIONIST: Who buys what? We have several executives who each purchase for their own departments.

SALESMAN: Well, I want the one who buys typewriters.

RECEPTIONIST: That would be our general manager. I am sorry, but he only sees representatives by appointment.

SALESMAN: O.K. I'll write then.

Couldn't happen? But that has been taken from a recording. It is the conversation almost word for word.

In the pre-approach find the name of the correct buyer before your call.

Scene III. A Retail Shop

SALESMAN: Good morning, Miss Jones. I have just got a repeat order for the twin-sets that have sold so well. I persuaded Mr. Smith to put in an extra 6/12ths canary— it's the new colour. They should go well, don't you think?

Miss Jones sniffs.

SALESMAN (aside to second assistant): What's the matter with her?

SECOND ASSISTANT: You called her Miss Jones. She told you last time you were here that she's Mrs. Jones, and she also told you that the new canary shade doesn't sell here.

A card-index system is essential to the Pre-approach. Salesmen of consumer goods are so sure they know everything about their regular customers that they feel there is no need to keep such records. But salesmen often make mistakes —especially in human relations because they have bad memories. The help that can be given by an assistant has been mentioned. Buyers listen to members of their staff. Managing directors are swayed by their secretaries, and works managers by shop foremen. So keep up-to-date records, with the names of assistants, their special preferences, whether they are married or single, when they take holidays, and so on.

Scene IV. An Accountant's Office

SALESMAN: Good morning, Mr. Smith, I wanted to talk to you about the enquiry you sent us.

ACCOUNTANT: I've told you several times not to call on Mondays. It is most inconvenient. You should have telephoned for an appointment.

In the Pre-approach, find the best time to call. This may not apply to canvassing salesmen, or men selling consumer goods, but it does apply to most representatives selling capital equipment.

Scene V. A Public House

SALESMAN: The Spurs are a wonderful club. They'll just walk over Fulham on Saturday.

PUBLICAN: Now that's where you're wrong. You haven't got the faintest idea what football is about. Man for man, Fulham are the far better team. ....

In the Pre-approach learn something of the background of a prospect. The salesman thought that the publican must be a Spurs supporter because his premises were close to the ground. He should have found out before calling, or avoided the subject of football altogether.

Scene VI. An Office

SALESMAN: Well, that's the whole proposition. I'm glad you are so interested, and I am sure you'd like to tie everything up now. I'll just write down the details. ....

OFFICE MANAGER: No, don't do that! I'm sorry, but I'm not in a position to buy. You'll have to see our general manager.

In the Pre-approach, find out as much as possible about a company's personnel and the authority of each executive to place orders. Is the company a limited liability company, or is it a partnership? If the latter, does one partner have the right to buy without consulting the other? If a manufacturer, does he make quality or cheap products? How many employees? What is the firm's credit rating?

All these questions need not be answered every time, but the more information a salesman can gather, the more success he will have in turning a prospect into a customer.

OBTAINING INFORMATION

There is a mine of information awaiting the salesman who will trouble to dig for it.

Head office

What do his company's sales executives know of a customer? Sometimes they have a great deal of information, but they do not give it to representatives without being asked. Ask!

Local traders

The speciality salesman making anything from ten to twenty calls a day cannot check prospective customers with head office. But local traders will often talk about their neighbours. Even if a salesman is unsuccessful at a call, he can still ask for information. He may say:

"Can you tell me the name of the proprietor of the butcher shop opposite?"
"Has he been there long?"
"What kind of man is he?"
"Has he a partner?"

The answers will help him make a good approach to that butcher.

Newspapers

Salesmen should read more newspapers. A representative selling high-priced equipment should read the city pages. He will learn of new developments, of the background of top executives, and new plans for expansion. In company reports he will find further information to help him talk in terms of the customer's interests.

The salesman selling to smaller traders should get local newspapers. There may be nothing useful in them for twenty-five weeks out of twenty-six, but on the twenty-sixth week there may be something that will indicate a sales opportunity at a local factory or local government office.

A shopkeeper is always pleased when a representative mentions his advertisement in the *Walling Gazette*, or what the editor of the *Blankton Star* wrote of his special window display, or a reference to his speech at the opening of an old people's home.

Some salesmen do better than others because they take their jobs more seriously. It is time-consuming to read local newspapers, but such time, spent in preparation for an order, is always worth while.

Trade magazines can also inform a salesman. It is wrong to believe that everyone who reaches the top must be either a genius or related to the company chairman. Nepotism is dying out, and private companies are taken over nearly every day. Public companies increase in size, with city editors ready to pounce at the least sign of inefficiency or a fall in profits. Chairmen are reluctant to bring in Nephew James, unless Nephew James is worthy of an executive post. As for genius, one or two top men may possess it, but I haven't met them. The men who get to the top give that little bit extra—extra study of a project, extra homework, extra thought to a sales drive, extra care with a new production programme, extra courage, extra effort to sell abroad, and so on. Most people don't want to sacrifice their time to 'extras'. They want success without effort, and it cannot be got.

Those salesmen who learn this lesson of the Pre-approach and study newspapers and magazines are laying the ground-work for future success.

Directories

New directories seem to be launched every week. At our offices details of new publications with up-to-date information about companies and company directors are received regularly. No salesman could be expected to buy these sets of directories, but they are nearly always available at local libraries. In directories you can find:

Names of directors of companies.
Scholastic background of directors.
Names and addresses of companies within a group.
Products manufactured or sold by a division of an organisation.
Capital structure.
Number of employees.

Observation

Good observation plays a part in the *Pre-approach*. A change of name over a shop front, or a good window display can help a salesman to surmount the first hurdle of the approach. The store buyer's preferences may be seen in the range of goods in the windows. It might be too late to obtain a contract when it is seen that a site is being levelled for a new building, but there could still be opportunities with the building director or developer. The salesman can learn something from the type of car parked outside an office or shop, from the décor of a waiting-room, from the letter-heading of a company's notepaper, from advertising campaigns, from the general staff atmosphere. Observation is essential in the *Pre-approach*.

Other salesmen

Salesmen are, by nature, talkative. Analytical chemists or accountants do not talk a great deal about their work, but salesmen are always ready to describe victories or defeats. Listeners, we know, can always learn something, and other salesmen can be surprisingly helpful. Many a useful hint has been picked up from their idle chatter at the end of the day.

They will refer to the peculiarities of customers, the ease with which a receptionist can be out-manoeuvred, the new machinery being installed in a certain factory, a new shop being opened. . .

No honourable salesman would get information from a competitor who might be ignorant of his reason for asking. But representatives selling non-competitive goods have much to teach. A salesman of office machinery may have noticed that new partitioning is needed. A salesman of books may know of a new store department for cosmetics.

Make friends with other salesmen. They can be good friends to you.

The Pre-approach data sheet

Your pre-approach inquiries must be recorded on a journey card or data sheet. For instance, a salesman of fire extinguishers may assemble all the facts likely to help him at a factory, and his data sheet will be:

Name of Company:	Jones Motors Ltd.
Address:	Meadowland, Kent
Telephone:	Kent 12345
Associate Companies:	Boon & Boon Ltd., Topworth, Essex.
Authority to buy:	Managing Director F. D. Jones.
Influence in buying:	Works Manager S. R. Smith.
Employees:	In Kent, about 150; In Essex, 130
Present System:	Units installed about 12 years ago. Cannot find out name of manufacturer. It seems that service is given irregularly.
Fire Hazards:	The usual, but special risk in warehouse where employees are allowed to smoke. Cigarette ends seen on floor. Should be influenced by fire recently at nearby mill.

Details of buying
   authority: M. Dir. Chairman of local Conser-
vative Association. Played cricket
for local team. Anti-blood sports.
Has son in business in Accounts
Dept. (Accounts Dept. on top floor
—fire risk.)
Married, but widower.
Self-made man and proud of it.
Works. Man. been with Co. 20
years. Loyal.
Thinks very little of salesmen.
Likes facts.
Member of local Dramatic Society.

Other Details: Must see Man. Dir. but will first
see Works Man. and tell him of
appointment with Man. Dir. Must
get his interest in first place.
Must be large order or nothing. Co.
may shortly seek stock exchange
quotation. What would happen if
fire before then?

Such a detailed sheet is worth while only when big business
is sought. If many factories are canvassed for £10–£20
orders, this intense study of a prospect and his business is
hardly necessary. But, with names changed, the data sheet is
very similar to one written by a fire-extinguisher salesman.
He is always out for big business and he gets it. He told me that
he is the only salesman in his organisation who goes to such
trouble, and his colleagues wonder how he pulls off such
large orders. They think his customers made initial inquiries, which they did not. He sets his sights on a few
factories each week. Then he carries out his research, telephones for an appointment, or calls cold. In the example
quoted, he got an order for over £1000-worth of fire-fighting
equipment. The average order taken by other salesmen in his
company is about £20.

Do you want more proof of the value of the *Pre-approach*?

OBTAINING THE INTERVIEW

It is wise to be armed with every scrap of information that can help you to close an order. It is right to plan your sales presentation. It is correct to check with your office before a call. But these preparations are wasted if a prospective buyer won't see you.

Representatives who sell to single retail shops have no problem getting an interview. The shopkeeper is nearly always available, and, if he is not busy with a queue of customers, he will see every salesman. Interviews are hard to get when a buyer is well guarded.

Managing directors, works manager, general managers, publicity managers, advertising managers, store buyers, and buyers for chains of retail shops are not visible when the salesman makes his entrance. They are in their offices, and between them and the salesman are assistants, secretaries, receptionists, commissionaires—all ready to bar the way.

Whether a salesman is seen by a company executive largely depends on his need for the goods being offered. The salesman must see that every prospective buyer is awakened to his need for the product or service. To do this, he must break down the barriers keeping him from the buyer's office.

How can a salesman get the maximum number of interviews?

Write a letter

Most tyro salesmen believe that a letter requesting an appointment is the proper and ethical way to approach a buyer. This might be true if there were a sellers' market in their products, but those days are past and seldom recur. After the last war, salesmen did not even need to write for appointments; buyers were begging them to call. Under competitive conditions, letters are a waste of time for most salesmen.

Let us examine them more closely. A blind-shot direct-mail advertising campaign saturates an area or a trade with letters in the hope that some of the recipients will be interested. If such a campaign gets a 1% response, that is average. Replies usually range from 0·5% to 2·5%.

Most campaigns of this kind ask the prospective buyer to send for further details or for samples. If a DMA shot were to invite appointments for representatives, there would probably not be even a 0·5% response.

If we take 1% as an average response to a well-designed and carefully conceived campaign, what chance has a salesman of improving on it? How many salesmen can have letters perfectly typed or perfectly facsimiled? Imagine writing 100 letters to try and get one appointment!

Unless the demand for your product far exceeds the supply, or unless it embodies some technical aspect of great interest to engineers, then don't waste time writing letters for appointments. Buyers can get similar goods from a hundred and one other suppliers and will not bother to reply to your letter.

Telephoning

Making appointments by telephone depends on the product or services you are selling and your own ability to use the instrument effectively. With many potential customers in an area, it is often a waste of time to try to make appointments by telephone. It is just as easy to call on prospects or customers.

Our own group of companies has this telephone policy:

The Industrial Division has about 200 men selling heating, ventilating and air-purifying units direct to shops, offices and factories. They rarely, if ever, use the telephone to make an appointment. With so many prospects available to them, if one call fails, another that may be more profitable can be made only minutes later. Telephoning would waste time.

We have another Division selling domestic appliances to retailers. Its salesmen do not use the telephone. They just call.

In a third Division, however, a smaller sales force of technical representatives sell a wide range of air filters, air diffu-

10

sers, ventilation plant, and switchgear to factories, hotels, power houses, atomic plants, and so on. Orders range from a few hundred pounds up to £100,000 and more. These men call direct on some factories, but most of their business comes through consulting engineers or architects. Many representatives cover wide areas and so may use the telephone to make appointments. They also make cold calls.

Tack Publications publish a marketing magazine, which has experienced advertising representatives to sell space. They do not call cold, but all appointments are made for them by telephone. A skilled telephone salesman does it.

In our London Sales Training Division, clients are usually visited by our own executive staff only by appointment. The telephone is used extensively for this purpose. However, men who represent our Training Division in the provinces tell us that it is just as rewarding to make cold calls as telephone appointments. But this may be due to our reputation, and the friendly relationship existing between our clients and the members of our training Division.

If the maximum number of customers or prospective customers can be seen by cold calls, there is very little reason to use the telephone. It is so easy for a prospect to turn down an appointment over the telephone or to replace the receiver quickly.

If you can use the telephone effectively and fill your days with appointments, this is the best method for you. Many salesmen, however, waste time seeking appointments on the telephone when they could be making calls to better advantage.

How to make an appointment on the telephone

You must speak confidently and clearly over the telephone. You may think you possess all the virtues and techniques necessary to hold telephone conversations, but you should check on this. Few people use the telephone to its best advantage. Some hold the mouthpiece so far away that they aren't on speaking terms with it. Others bark, or growl, or dry up, or talk too much, or speak so softly that most of what they say goes unheard. Men who sound rude and brusque over the telephone may be charming people to meet.

So check your own telephone manner. Ask a friend how you sound to him on the telephone. If you cannot use the telephone effectively, train yourself, and improve your technique.

1. Hold the mouthpiece about one inch from your lips. Otherwise your voice may not be audible.

2. Have a notebook and pencil handy to write down names, times or dates.

3. Find out the name of the person you want and then ask for him.

4. Sound businesslike, cheerful, and enthusiastic. Put a smile into your voice. Never give the impression that although you are asking for an appointment, you don't really believe that you will achieve your aim.

5. Work out a brief sales presentation so that you know exactly how you are going to convince someone that they should give you an appointment. You have few—very few—words in which to convince your prospect that he should give you an appointment. Make sure that every word counts. The rules for building a sequence are the same as for a full sales story.

6. Your time is just as valuable as the prospect's; to you it is more valuable. Decide how many prospects you can see in a day. Try to work a small area to save travelling time. Arrange convenient appointments. You may not win every time, but you will win more often than you lose. You may fix appointments for 9 a.m., 10.15, 11.30, followed by lunch and perhaps a journey, and again for 2 p.m., 3.10, 4.30 and 6. Salesmen who made only three appointments a day have doubled this number by working to a schedule.

7. To get convenient appointments, say this:

> "Mr. Jones, you will, I feel sure, like to hear how the Office and Shops Act can help you increase business in your retail shops. The new form of lighting I want to talk to you about complies with the Act, and will also attract customers to your counters. . . ."

Now ask for the appointment. Here are alternatives:

(a) Salesman: "When may I call to see you?"
    Prospect: "Well, I'm very busy just now. Put it in writing."

(b) Salesman: "May I call to see you some time next week?"
    Prospect: "No, I shall be away. Telephone me again later."

(c) Salesman: "May I call at 10 a.m.?"
    Prospect: "Sorry, I shall be tied up then. Drop me a line."

(d) Salesman: "Would you prefer to see me at 9.10 to-morrow or would 9.50 suit you better?"
    Prospect: "Make it 9.10."

When asking for an appointment, suggest alternative times. If the prospect says: "I won't be here tomorrow," suggest the same times for another day.

Sometimes it is wise to use the diminishing alternative, as follows:

> "Would you like to see me this week or next week?"
> "Next week."
> "Would Monday or Tuesday suit you better?"
> "Tuesday."
> "And would 2 o'clock or 2.50 be better for you on Tuesday?"

Most salesmen ask for an appointment at the hour or half-hour. By suggesting odd times to those usually booked for appointments, you can win two victories. First, you can give the impression that you are very busy and are squeezing in the prospect. Second, by changing the traditional appointment time, you may influence the prospect away from his traditional refusal to make an appointment.

8. With a particularly difficult prospect, ask for a specified time to outline your proposal briefly. For example:

"Mr. Brown, I appreciate how busy you are, but it is busy men who appreciate our proposition. You won't waste your time if you see me. Please let me prove this to you. Just give me ten minutes. When I arrive I promise you that I shall place my watch on your desk. If after ten minutes you are not interested in my proposition, then I shall pick up my watch and go. That's fair, isn't it? When would you prefer me to call, Mr. Brown? At 8.50 or 11.15?"

9. If the prospect still refuses to give an interview, you have one final card to play:

"Very well, Mr. Brown. Then let me leave the matter open. Next month I shall call on you and take a chance that you will be able to see me. I am sure you will remember this brief conversation and will give me an interview."

This puts Mr. Brown under a small obligation to you. It may be slight, but it could help you to be seen when you are in the district next time.

If your product or service is suitable for selling by appointment, the telephone can be a boon. Make sure you know how to use it correctly.

Visiting cards

Even salesmen who rarely use them are attached to their cards, and they have their uses.

A buyer who sees many salesmen cannot be expected to remember every name. But if he has the visiting card before him, sent in by the receptionist, he can refresh his mind by glancing at it and so pronounce the name correctly.

Sometimes a customer asks for a card. It may then go straight into the waste-paper basket, it may not. Rather than apologise for not having one, carry a card.

However, a card will not break down barriers. The rule is: If you can always get an appointment by sending through your card, then keep a good supply. You are lucky to represent a company with its products in such demand. But if you have frequently called on a prospect, each time sending up your card and each time failing in your mission, you must work to a different plan.

The card might show the name of a company—Johnson's (Household) Ltd. for example. A buyer glances at it and being satisfied with his present suppliers, returns it with the message: "Nothing today." But the salesman representing Johnson's (Household) Ltd. might have a line which would interest that buyer; this cannot be learned from the card.

Perhaps the card lists some of a company's products. With the company name—Mason's Office Suppliers Ltd. might be listed the equipment sold, typewriters, duplicators, carbon papers, ribbons, and so on. The office manager might feel that he does not need any of these, for the card does not tell a sales story. The duplicator may work faster than any other makes, it may have special inking features, and, most important of all, it may take a large size of paper. But how could the manager know all this by looking at a card? Again he will return the message: "Nothing today."

Thousands of salesmen make thousands of abortive calls, because they persist in using cards that are misleading.

Here is a technique which usually works and, however often it is used, brings about interviews.

You go into a reception office, guarded by a young telephonist. It is essential that you walk briskly up to the reception desk. If you have a hangdog look or appear ill-at-ease, you won't succeed even in the first part of your task, which is to convey a sense of the importance of your visit to the receptionist.

You smile and say: "Good morning. Will you please tell Mr. Brown that Mr. Heyworth is here to see him?" Then spell your name: "H-e-y-w-o-r-t-h."

After this, walk right away from the receptionist's desk. Don't indicate that you expect a question from her. If you hesitate, you are lost, because she will probably ask: "What is your business?"

She must then decide whether to ask your business or to telephone Mr. Brown and tell him that Mr. Heyworth is in the waiting-room to see him. She has no idea of the importance of your visit. You might be a client, or a friend of the buyer. On most occasions that you make this approach, the receptionist will telephone Mr. Brown and give him your message.

When Mr. Brown gets it, he has two choices. He can ask the telephonist: "Will you please find out what he wants?" or he can say: "Tell him to come up and see me."

Most Mr. Browns take the second course because they cannot identify Mr. Heyworth. He may be someone they have met. He may have made an appointment which they have forgotten.

When the receptionist asks for information, you must give it. If she then telephones Mr. Brown, you must try to speak to him yourself.

When you walk away from the reception desk, the telephonist should ring the buyer. As she picks up the telephone, you come back to the desk and stand close by, so that when she says: "Mr. Brown has asked the reason for your visit," you can put out your hand and ask if you may speak to Mr. Brown. Here again you will find that, if you make a display of determination, the telephonist will hand the telephone to you. Now it is up to you to convince Mr. Brown in a minute or two that he should see you.

This technique, therefore, gives you many opportunities,

none of which are possible when you use a card. You will find that you will get at least two interviews from every four calls by using this kind of approach.

The secretary

Mr. Brown, of course, could send down his secretary to see you. Never try to be clever with a secretary, or think that flattery will win her over. She is much too astute.

Here is an article written by my own secretary, Mrs. Gordon, who has been with me for 27 years, for one of our magazines:

"One of my duties as secretary is, of course, to be my boss's watchdog, to make sure that nobody gets into his office unless it is someone he wants to see. And very, very few men get past me! Imagine the constant string of callers all asking to see my boss. Half my time is spent in probing gently: 'What is it about? Yes, I appreciate that it is a private matter, but the managing director is not available just now, and if you just give me some small indication. . .' You know it all. Thousands of secretaries every day all over the country are watching their employers' interests just as keenly.

"I think I know all the angles now. In the early days I may have let one or two slip past me with 'It's a private matter that I can only discuss with him.' Nowadays, however, that cuts no ice.

"But YOU must get in to see the man who matters. How do you do it?

"Do you know what I do with all the business cards that are handed to me by men trying to sell something to my boss? The managing director never sees them. I have a large waste-paper basket!

"Telephone for an appointment? All calls are put through to me and I soon sift out those to whom my employer will not want to talk. 'Yes, I shall certainly give him your message when he returns. . .'

"But, in spite of all my vigilance, there are always two ways of getting past me.

"In the first place, when I come down to see you, do appreciate that I know a great deal about the business. Even secretaries who have not been long in their jobs quickly grasp the ramifications of a business. It is wrong, therefore, to try and fob me off with a story that you have something special that you must show to the boss personally and which you cannot disclose to anyone else. It is no use being secretive. I know that you have been taught that it is a waste of time telling your sales story to a person who cannot buy. I know that it is a rule that, if you tell such a story, the person will certainly not relay it to the buyer in a proper selling manner. But when faced with a secretary you have no alternative. Therefore tell me briefly about your proposition. Tell me how it can help my boss, or the company. If you really sell me well enough and convince me that your arguments are right, the chances are that I will put in a good word for you and get you that appointment. If you fail to do this— and there can be many reasons for your failure—my boss's time will be fully booked for weeks ahead, and I have to keep a very close eye on his appointment book—then you must try the alternative. It was used by a man called Smith, who had been calling steadily for quite a while.

"At first I used all the usual excuses: 'I'm so sorry, Mr. Smith, the managing director is out, away, in conference...'

"He was always extremely polite and pleasant, but eventually, after several calls, I tried to avoid him. I wasn't in my office when he called, and my boss was out too. Then I would send out a message to him that the managing director was not available. But it was no use. One day the reply came back: 'Would I see him for just one minute, even though my chief was not available?'

"In sheer desperation I asked him to wait a minute, and I went in to my boss and begged him to see Mr. Smith. A quarter of an hour later Mr. Smith came out beaming, having booked a very sizeable order for equipment that my boss had been considering for some time. Mr. Smith taught me a lesson. I hope he may have taught you one, too. *Polite persistence pays.*"

Here are rules to remember for obtaining more interviews:

1. Treat receptionists with respect to obtain their co-operation.
2. Don't wait about too long. Your time is valuable. If someone is going to keep you waiting for thirty or forty minutes, it may pay you better to make a call elsewhere.
3. If there is any reading matter relating to the firm's activities in the reception office, study it while you are waiting.
4. If you are kept waiting a little while, don't keep worrying the receptionist.
5. Don't try to act the great lover with secretaries. Familiarity will only breed contempt for you.
6. If it will help you to convince a secretary that you should have an appointment, give her a piece of sales literature that is easily understood and which she can, if necessary, show to her boss.
7. When a secretary comes into the waiting-room, don't forget to stand up.
8. The more you learn about the pre-approach, the easier it will be for you to obtain more interviews. Your success depends on the number of interviews.
9. A secretary will appreciate words like: "I should be grateful for your help," or "I wonder if you could help me." Most people like to help others.

DIFFICULT BUYERS

Pre-approach planning must include techniques for handling every kind of customer or prospect. If thought is not given to this, a salesman may meet a situation he is unable to tackle.

Most buyers are reasonable people who can be influenced by a good sales presentation and by human relations. Some will order; others will have different reasons for refusing to buy. Few salesmen take large orders from everyone they call upon. But the main difference between the good and the average representative is that the first-class man gets extra orders from customers with whom the average salesman can make little headway.

If this is true for the run-of-the-mill buyer who makes perhaps 80% of all contacts made, it is even more true for buyers who make life hard for the salesman. With these difficult prospects and customers the average salesman will fail more frequently than he will succeed because he won't know how to win them over to his side. Even the very experienced representative must work much harder for his orders when a buyer does all he can to put him off.

Why are some buyers so difficult? The main reason is fear of salesmen, allied to fear of making a mistake. To frustrate a salesman, a buyer develops an act.

When you meet difficult buyers, you must be prepared to handle them correctly.

Mr. Talker

We know that a salesman lives by the words he uses. If he is not allowed to give his presentation, how can he close an order? To prevent a salesman from completing his sales sequence, one type of buyer talks endlessly. He talks on any subject. The salesman may mention a window display and the buyer will be off, talking about the dozens of displays he has contrived and the displays of his competitors. The sale is bogged down. The salesman, believing in human relations, may ask the prospect if he enjoyed his holiday; that prospect will talk about the holiday for so long that there is little

time left for selling. There is only time for the prospect to say:
"See me when you call again next time."

This type of prospect or customer will sidetrack the salesman in all sorts of ways. He will talk about politics, the
weather, his favourite hobby, other people in the locality.
Whenever the salesman tries to return to selling, he cannot
stem the flow of words. While the salesman must not be a
pouncer and interrupt a buyer, there is a vast difference
between pouncing and allowing a buyer to talk him through
the door. With Mr. Talker, a salesman must pounce. He
must stop him talking so that he can assert himself. He must
interrupt the prospect without offending him. Wait until the
talker says something that can be linked to a sales point. It
might be the weather. The talker might be explaining how
rain has affected his business. He might be giving a weather
report stretching over the last thirty years. The salesman
must interrupt with:

> "Excuse me, Mr. Brown, for just one moment, but you
> have said something which is so interesting and I know you
> will now agree with what I have to say. It is when the
> weather is bad and your customers sit at home that you
> have to do something to bring them into the shop. This is
> where I can help you. . ."

The talker may be interminably describing some tech-
nicality of his manufacturing process. He is bogging the
salesman down in technical details. The salesman must interrupt loudly with:

> "May I say that it is obvious why you are technically so
> far ahead of your competitors, but I can help you not only
> to go further ahead but to beat them on price, because. . ."

The salesman must never be timid with the talker, because he will keep quiet only when he feels he is in the presence of a stronger personality than his own.

Mr. Too-friendly

A buyer may be abrupt, curt, almost rude, but he may also listen to a salesman's proposition. The brusque buyer is not too difficult a man to overcome, but the too-friendly buyer can make life very hard for the salesman. He seems to agree with everything he is told, but does so in a facile way. He suggests that he is agreeing halfheartedly and out of politeness, but has no intention of buying. This kind of buyer will greet a salesman in a friendly manner, will be ready with a smile, will pat a salesman on the back. But his pleasant manner is a disguise. He wants to be difficult. He knows it is hard for a salesman to get down to tough selling when he is being so friendly. The timid salesman is always impressed with friendliness. He doesn't try to close an order. He will write on his report to head office:

"Mr. Brown greeted me in a most friendly way. He listened to everything I had to say and I am sure he agreed with our proposition. He would not come to a decision, but he is undoubtedly a very good prospect and I feel sure that next time I call I will get an order."

But he won't get an order. The prospect will be just as friendly on the next occasion. "I told you last time how much I agree with everything you say. But this isn't the right time for me to stock your products. I certainly will one day, don't have any fear of that."

This will happen at every call. It takes a strong salesman to overcome the too-friendly buyer; only the strong salesman will put his foot down and start to sell. If the customer agrees with him, he will ask for the order. When he doesn't agree, he will sell even more strongly. The salesman knows this buyer for what he is worth, and he will not be shown to the door with the buyer's arm around his shoulder, being thanked for calling. The only thanks he wants for calling is the signed order.

Even at the risk of antagonising this new friend, the strong salesman will carry on with his sequence. You must win the friendship of a buyer, who should prefer you to competitors' salesmen, but proof of his friendship can come only when he gives you orders.

Mr. Timid

This one never seems to make up his mind. He cannot come to a decision, avoids making it, and should not be a buyer at all. The more timid the buyer, the more decisive the salesman must be. Do not give him alternatives. His mind must be made up for him. He must be given a single course of action, and induced to take it.

The timid buyer's greatest anxiety is that he will make a mistake. This can be understood in a very small business, where a mistake may cause considerable financial embarrassment. But store buyers too, can be timid. They are scared of the merchandising manager's displeasure if they purchase the wrong stock. They are frightened of overstocking. They are scared to open new accounts. They want only to buy samples, and, having sold them, they want to buy more samples. They rarely have the courage to place a large order unless past experience shows that the goods will readily sell.

Much time must be spent on building Mr. Timid's confidence, confidence in the salesman, confidence in his products. This must be accompanied by tremendous enthusiasm. If the salesman is unenthusiastic he doesn't stand a chance of selling to the timid buyer; if he keeps up his enthusiasm some of it will eventually rub off on Mr. Timid, who will start to feel enthusiastic about the products and summon the courage to place a fair-sized order. Talk to Mr. Timid of larger quantities than you hope to sell; he may be frightened at first, but when you suggest the smaller order, he will be relieved and more inclined to buy.

Mr. Strong-and-silent

Years ago the hero of most novels was a strong and silent

man. Girls seemed to like this masculine type, but now they prefer someone with a little intellect who can talk rationally on many subjects.

The strong and silent man is a relic of the past, but he can still be found amongst buyers. He is a difficult proposition. While the talker won't stop talking, his opposite number won't say anything. When the salesman explains one of his most important selling features, the only answer is a grunt. And if you can't get him to open out, you can't sell to him.

You must make this kind of prospect agree with you. He must be brought into the sale. Even the most vociferous sales-man cannot overcome the strong and silent buyer. His words will dry up. Many salesmen tail away under the baleful gaze of the silent prospect. The way to succeed is to sell in a series of questions. Practically every sentence must be a question. At first the answer may be a grunt, but eventually the pros-pect must say something. He might be able to grunt a half-dozen times, but on the seventh occasion, tough as he is, the prospect must speak, especially if the question is controver-sial. If the answer is a straightforward "yes" it need not be taken further. If it is "no", the salesman should invite elab-oration. He must be as tough as the strong silent buyer, saying something like:

"You are not being fair to yourself or to me, sir, when you just answer 'no'. Why don't you think that this tool will help your production?"

Ask questions, and soon the strong and silent type will begin to talk. When he starts talking, you know you are making progress with the sale.

Mr. Pompous

There are pompous people everywhere, but some buyers are so self-important that they are more pompous than most. They are conscious of their authority and their hold over a salesman; they have him at their mercy. They are often fawned upon by weak salesmen. They are tin gods of their little empires. They enjoy showing off to the staff at the expense of the salesman. If Mr. Pompous should be a factory manager, he struts amongst the machinery in his workshops, his every step indicating his sense of his own importance.

You cannot win over this prospect by deflating him, by making him appear unimportant. A salesman cannot diminish him by building himself up, by pointing out that other firms place large orders for his goods. This makes the prospect feel less important and antagonises him because he cannot equal those big orders. And if you deflate him, you are finished. You must build him up, make him feel even more important than he is. Congratulate him on the way his department is run, if it is well administered. If his factory is efficient, praise him for it. If he is known as a keen buyer, tell him that everyone knows he is a keen buyer. If he will often make a quick decision, tell him that he has the reputation of a man who, once he has made up his mind, will take action and buy. The only way to tackle Mr. Important is to convince him that you share his belief in himself.

Mr. Bluffer

The bluffer is similar to Mr. Timid at heart. He deceives salesmen. He talks in large quantities, stresses that he buys in thousands but he doesn't make a decision. Again, the salesman reports to his company:

> "I was with Mr. Brown today, and I am confident that he will soon give me the biggest order I have ever obtained. He is interested in our products, and is thinking of buying 200 gross."

The poor salesman has been misled. He won't get any orders from Mr. Bluffer, although he may have said: "I don't believe in playing about. When I buy, I buy. It is not worth my opening an account with you for just a few gross. In six months' time I should be ready to give you a good order." This is all bluff. You must tie him down. He may want to place a small order but, having taken his stand, cannot easily reduce the quantity. Say to him:

"Mr. Johnson, I appreciate you want to buy 200 gross, but, if you take my advice, don't do this at first. Now I know you will think it very wrong of me to make this suggestion. 200 gross would not worry you but it would worry me. One of my biggest accounts began in quite a small way. The buyer is a man like you, who knows his own mind, but I asked him to test out the market and find for himself just how many he could sell in the course of six weeks. If you begin with ten gross. . ."

This is appreciated by the bluffer. You have called his bluff, but he doesn't know it. The chances are that you will get your small order, but if you think that in a month or two you will get a big contract, you will be sadly disillusioned. You must tie the bluffer down to a small quantity initially, even if it goes against the grain of a salesman after big business. The big business will come only after orders for smaller quantities. It will never come if no orders are placed.

Mr. Stubborn

When the stubborn buyer has made up his mind, nothing seems to budge him. Any hint of criticism will lose the order. He would rather make a wrong decision than change his mind. His problem is psychological. He is afraid of appearing weak. If he has raised an objection, he doesn't want you to prove him wrong. He is the kind of man who will tell you that he always believes in admitting when he is in the wrong; unfortunately, he always believes he is in the right. The strength of your sales presentation enables you to sell to him. A presentation that forestalls objections, lets him feel he is making all the decisions all the time.

11

Mr. Busy-busy

The very busy buyer may be an office manager, works manager or the owner of a garage. If he runs a small garage, you will often find that he is working on a car, inside the bonnet or underneath, when you call. Never try to sell in this situation. Without his undivided attention, go on your way. But, likely as not, your next call will find him as busy as before.

Similarly an office manager will ask you in, offer you a seat, ask for details of your proposition but before you can say a word he is on the telephone giving urgent instructions.

There is a series of interruptions. First, "Miss Brown, will you bring in those files now?" As you open your mouth: "I am sorry, just wait a minute, will you?" And he presses the intercommunication button to speak to some member of his staff. When you begin again, you notice he is not even looking at you, but examining papers. He may be a works manager and you trot after him through the works. He talks to this man, and to that. He makes for the stores, starts to listen to you, and then decides he has another job to do. Such busy, busy people! They are busy because they are inefficient. They are putting on an act to impress you, and also an act to get rid of you. You must stand firm with such people. If the garage owner is under a car, say: "Could I just show you this?" Don't get down to his level, but wait until he comes up from the car before you show him anything.

The best way to tackle this difficult buyer is to sympathise with the amount he has to do. That, after all, is the explanation behind his act. Say to him: "Mr. Johnson, I don't know how you do it. Are you on the go like this all the time? Don't you ever have a break?"

This will probably bring a change of atmosphere. "Well," he may answer, "I am kept pretty busy." He has made his point, and now he will usually listen to you. Remember, then, that Mr. Busy is trying to impress you. Once he knows you are impressed, he is more ready to listen to your sales presentation.

Mr. Mrs. or Miss Shy

Salesmen are not generally shy, but I have known a few who were, when not selling. Someone who buys regularly might be expected to lose all sense of shyness, but many buyers are shy. A man who buys engineerings products is not inevitably an extrovert. He may have begun at the bench and worked his way up, but stayed shy. This is especially true of women buyers. Some are arrogant and tough, but others are rarely at ease with salesmen. The shy buyer will seldom look you in the face, and his eyes will wander disconcertingly around the room. He must be closely involved in the sale, and this can be done by asking questions, or by using pencil and notepad. As you develop your sales presentation, write down some of the features and show them to the buyer for his agreement. If calculations are required, make them with the shy buyer. Make a deliberate mistake and allow him to spot it. This technique will overcome his shyness.

Mr. Sarcastic

The sarcastic buyer may have a warped sense of humour or a difficult home life. If he is under the thumb of his wife, he boosts his authority in sarcasm towards salesmen and colleagues. He delights in making the salesman feel small. He comments caustically upon your sales kit, your company, salesmen in general. He interrupts your sales presentation with some foolish remark that may raise a laugh from one of his assistants.

He is at the top of his form with an audience—an assistant buyer, an assistant in a shop, workpeople; he loves playing to an audience. If you quarrel with him, you will lose the account for good. You will be sorely tempted to do so, but a salesman should subdue such reactions against a prospective buyer. At all costs keep your temper. Try to smile at his sarcasm. Explain that you know how he feels about the company, but he is not quite correct because. . . . He is showing off, and probably using sarcasm in self-defence. Mr. Sarcastic may not be a bad fellow underneath and, if you persist without losing your temper you will eventually get an order from him. He won't stop being sarcastic, but his remarks will lose their sting when you get to know him better.

Mr. Old-and-Experienced

He will probably have been in business for many years, either on his own account or for others. He may not take kindly to new-fangled ideas, and he doesn't think highly of modern salesmanship. He lives in the past, when salesmen were more servile and he could, with more leisure, select the goods he required. He is often a kindly man and, although he may seem irritable occasionally, put it down to his having heard everything before, or to his health being less good than it once was. He always believes that the salesman is trying to put something over on him; talking down to him will lose any chance of an order.

Do not be clever with this man. Never produce the slick answer. You must respect him for what he is and for what he has done. You may not see eye to eye with him, but he has vast experience in his line of business. Learn from that experience. Ask his advice. Show him that you are ready to learn from him much more than he can learn from you. Impress him with your integrity and honesty. Never try to rush him, or force an issue. Prove each point step by step. Do not judge him by appearances. He is not like Mr. Sarcastic. He may look gruff and frightening, but he could develop into a great friend. You can depend upon this buyer more than upon the up-and-coming young man who changes his suppliers almost as often as he changes his suits.

Mr. Young-and-Foolish

This is the most difficult buyer, the young man who has

risen too quickly. He does not know that he is foolish, and does not like to be told that he is young. He may have a beard to make him look older. He is worried, but he tries to hide it. He would hate you to think him young and inexperienced. He is scared of making a mistake that would prompt a relative or his chief to wonder if it was right to give such a young man an important position.

One day he will learn his business and carry out his job efficiently. Now it is your duty to help him by giving him a complete sales presentation and so teach him about your products; he then learns more about the goods he is selling. If you are older, take care to show him the greatest courtesy and do not imply that your experience is superior to his. At the same time let him teach you something so that you can thank him for his help. You must make him feel less young and inexperienced. This way you will sell to him and make a good friend of him.

Help your customers

When planning the pre-approach, remember that you can sell to most people once. To keep a customer he must buy from you more than once. Try and understand his idiosyncrasies. If your customer is a retailer, plan your pre-approach to include advice on disposing of his goods. Be a good example to your customers. The salesman is a mirror, and he reflects the customer. Don't swear if a customer does, and you will find he moderates his language. The bad-mannered customer will become polite by your example. Never prove him wrong. The argument that results doesn't lead to an order. Demonstrate that you are right, without putting him in the wrong.

If he makes a mistake, keep quiet about it. He needs to save face in front of his assistants.

The good salesman will look after his customers, nurse them, and try to satisfy them. Satisfied customers are unpaid salesmen for you. The pre-approach plan ensures that you see the most customers and give them the best service.

CHAPTER X

THE APPROACH

Have you noticed the recent change in the introduction of plays on television?

At one time they began with the title, following by the names of those contributing to the production—writer, make-up expert, hairdresser, dress designer, scene designer, wardrobe mistress, Uncle Tom Cobley and all. That wasn't all, we had the names of cameraman, producer, director, assistant director, and the assistant to the assistant. If we were not thoroughly browned off with this directory of production personnel, we would settle down to view. Occasionally we would switch to the other station and would not trouble to switch back.

But that has changed. If the play is due at 8.0 p.m. at 8.0 p.m. sharp we are given the opening scene. It may be a man in black following a blonde in white. We are intrigued and held, and only then is the title flashed on the screen. We don't switch to the other channel because we are eager to learn why the man in black is following the blonde.

Sometimes another technique is used. We see a number of swift scenes from the play, shown in the belief that at least one of them will interest us and prevent us from switching off. This new approach by T.V. planners keeps us away from the rival station.

There is nothing new in this. Think of the differences in book jackets and record sleeves. On the face of it, they should not be needed. Joe Snooks writes a first-class novel. He is a famous novelist and the book is well reviewed. But his publishers do not rely on his reputation. If they did they would merely wrap the book in brown paper and print on it only his name. But how many would select it at a bookstall? Joe

Snooks' publishers spend a lot of time and money to get the right jacket. They use skilled artists or designers, and approve the final cover after many trials. They know that their book competes for attention with hundreds of others, and they want to ensure that it gets it.

Joe Snooks, being a professional writer, knows that he must begin his story so persuasively that no one will want to put it down. One publisher has said that the opening sentences of a book can make or mar its success.

In every aspect of marketing, an advertisement, a sales brochure, or a sales presentation the first objective is to attract attention.

The formula for a sales presentation is A.I.D.A., which once stood for Attention, Interest, Desire, Action. The 'A' is now the Approach, and it is here that the salesman must get the undivided attention of his prospect or customer. Only by holding the attention is the salesman able to continue his story. He has a few fleeting seconds—about the time it takes for a match to burn itself out—to win the undivided attention of the buyer.

To understand this, put yourself in the shoes of the buyer. Whatever his business or position, the owner of a grocery shop, the works director of an engineering company, he will see many salesmen each day. Most of them have little interest for him, for he is probably satisfied with his regular suppliers. So the sooner he can get rid of a salesman, the sooner he can pursue his normal tasks. This may be wrong, for his main duty is to buy wisely, but he is rarely aware of this. He often looks upon a salesman as a necessary evil. Imagine, then, that you are such a buyer. A salesman approaches you. He rambles incoherently about his range of products. You will soon cut him short and send him on his way. He didn't win your undivided attention, and so you hardly heard his sales story.

Thousands of buyers do this every day. To surmount buyer apathy, a salesman must think hard about clinching his attention at the approach. First, he must be well turned out, for a slovenly salesman will not command attention. Second, he must arouse interest at the outset. The first two steps of the sale are closely connected. The approach and creation of interest are separated only because, however great the interest aroused by the approach, it must be maintained and increased during the next few minutes of the presentation.

Adverse conditions

Never try to make an approach in adverse conditions. Your approach sentence may be perfect and win the interest of the buyer, but you can rarely complete the sales approach to your advantage if conditions are not favourable.

For example, you might greet a shopkeeper while he is inspecting his window, which is being dressed. Your approach will fall on deaf ears. The prospect is then much more interested in his display than in you. You may well find yourself standing on the pavement, with a hearing refused, and the shopkeeper closing the shop door behind him. In this case, you must first get him back into the shop, before beginning to sell to him.

On another occasion you may meet a buyer as he is leaving his office. He has put on hat and coat, and seems to be in a hurry. If you make your approach he may say: "Tell me quickly what it is all about. I have a train to catch." Tell him nothing. Make an appointment when he is not so rushed for time. Do not try to sell in a corridor, but get the buyer back into his office. Say: "Can I come into your office, sir?" and move towards it. The buyer will usually follow you.

Try to avoid selling when a third party is present; buyers will play to the gallery, to your disadvantage.

When the shopkeeper is high up a ladder, checking his stock, don't begin to sell until he has climbed down to floor level. When the works manager is helping one of his staff with a problem, stand aside until he has given his advice and then try to lead him back to his office.

Every salesman has stories of sales conducted under adverse conditions. One may have taken an order when a customer was getting into his car. Another took an order in a bus queue. Yet another sold to a farmer while he was under a tractor. My favourite story concerns a sale I made when I was in a shop and the proprietor was ill in the back bedroom. His wife would not let me into his room. I shouted at him and he shouted back at me, and he finally signed the order I sent in to him. But these are exceptions. Make an effort to sell under adverse conditions when there is nothing to lose. If, for instance, you are calling in a district outside your normal territory and will probably not return there for a year or so, the attempt is worth making. In general, however, stick to the rule not to sell under adverse conditions.

Another rule

This is short and simple. Never say to a prospect or customer: "I was just passing by, so I thought I would call to see you." You are not a passer-by; you call with the specific object of obtaining an order. You call because you have benefits to offer the buyer. You do not call by chance in the hope that the buyer will be interested in you.

The sentence

As we have said, your sales presentation is constructed on a series of sentences that summarise the steps to the order—the approach, creation of interest, creation of confidence, the product's benefits, creation of desire, the close. You must first work out a good approach sentence for every call. But before this, you must decide on the type of approach you will use.

The introductory approach

The introductory approach is used by most salesmen, and, for this reason alone, it should be avoided whenever possible. All day long a buyer hears:

"I am from Smith's."

"I represent Wright's."

"I have called from Brown's."

If the company is a household name, this approach may be helpful. It may work in reverse. The buyer may have been let down by other divisions of your firm. He will hold it against every member of the group. He may know that the organisation offers only small discounts, and the salesman is involved in argument before he starts to sell. At the approach stage the buyer has little interest in a company name. He is only mildly interested in what a salesman has to offer. He has no interest whatsoever in the salesman's name. Here is another introductory approach:

"Good morning, Mr. Jones. My name is Smith and I represent White's."

Does the buyer care at the outset whether the salesman's name is Smith or Thistlewhaite? One New York buyer would invariably answer this approach with "So what?" This was most disconcerting. The approach could be taken this step further:

"Good morning, Mr. Jones. My name is Smith and I represent White's. We are agents for Atlas typewriters."

To which the immediate reply could be: "I don't need any typewriters."

The introductory approach can sometimes be used, but only if it helps to bring the buyer into the sale quickly. For example:

"Good morning, Mr. Smith. I am from Brown's. You have probably heard of. . ."

And the salesman might continue with "us," "our new department," "our new promotional campaign," "our new development". Or he may alter the approach slightly to conclude with the words: "You have probably seen our advertisement in the trade papers."

This approach does not stress any benefits, but it does invite the buyer to make an immediate reply instead of a refusal to learn more about the goods being offered. He can only answer "yes" or "no". If the answer is "yes" then the salesman would go on: "Then you know how much we can help you with . . ." (fast-moving stock, increased output, or greater efficiency). If the prospect answers "no", the salesman can still come back with: "Then you will certainly want to hear how we can help you to . . ."

This approach combines the introductory and the question approach. It gets over the disadvantage of the salesman introducing himself and then waiting for the prospect to show interest.

At this early stage of the sale, you are not asking the buyer's opinion of your goods. You are involving him in the sale and making him listen to your sales presentation.

The stunt approach

Stunt approaches were widely used in the "twenties". They are now infrequent, possibly because buyers are more sophisticated and do not take kindly to gimmicks. These approaches are mostly used by speciality salesmen, although they are often taught to salesmen of every product and service. Some sales executives are so struck with the need for dynamism that they reject ordinary means. They forget that a knowledge of the fundamentals of salesmanship is essential, and that very few men can use a stunt approach. When a buyer said: "I don't want your products," one sales manager would answer: "You've bloody well got to have them." Oddly enough he got away with it once or twice and got the notion that he did likewise at every call. It wasn't true, but he never tired of telling his salesmen that they should be similarly tough with prospects. He misled both himself and his men.

I knew a salesman of vending machines. His approach when he went into a prospect's shop, was to throw a handful of coins on the floor before he said a word. He would then say to the startled shop-owner: "You are throwing money away like this every minute of every day." He got away with it time after time, but hundreds of salesmen who were taught to copy him failed miserably.

It takes a very strong salesman to continue with his sales presentation after a stunt approach. A salesman of outdoor advertising signs made his approach by taking from his bag a piece of armour-plated glass and hitting it with a hammer. He would explain: "You cannot smash this glass. We use it to protect the most outstanding advertising sign ever developed." Unfortunately, less practised men would smash the glass and they soon gave up the stunt. The sales manager didn't know about this for many months. He was deluding himself.

A fire-extinguisher salesman used a gruesome picture of badly-burned children rescued from a house after a fire. "Would you like this to happen to your children?" he would ask at the approach. He told his sales director of his success with this approach and similar pictures were sent to the entire sales force. It was a complete failure. Most men found that the prospects were so upset by looking at the photographs that they were no longer interested in the sales presentation.

If you represent a company that teaches a stunt approach, my advice is don't use it. Only one salesman in a thousand can do so successfully. You can develop a more effective approach for yourself.

The factual approach

The entire sales sequence is based on facts, and customer benefits derive from them. At the approach the buyer isn't the least interested in the salesman or his products. His concern is only with the welfare of his business and of himself.

If, then, the first few words he hears from the salesman comprise an interesting factual statement that relates to his own business, he will want to hear more of the proposition. Here are some examples of the factual approach.

Watch-bracelets to jewellers

If you sold expanding watch-bracelets to jewellers, you would have a choice of approaches. But can you think of an unusual fact to help you at this stage of the sale? Even if you know very little about watch-bracelets, you may think of the ease with which the jeweller could fit the bracelet to a customer's wrist. So one opening would be:

"Good morning, Mr. Jeweller. Our expanding bracelets will help you satisfy most of your customers."

But is this a strong opening? Here is an approach used by one salesman of expanding bracelets with great success:

"Good morning, Mr. Jeweller. With every expanding watch-bracelet you sell there is a hidden extra 5% profit for you. I am from the Jewellery Corporation . . ."

He then elaborates his sales story by telling the jeweller that a standard make of bracelet may require alteration to fit the customer's wrist. This extra service is time-wasting for no charge can be made for it. The salesman then explains that no such service is needed with his expanding bracelet, which adjusts itself. That gives the hidden profit to the jeweller, a profit derived from the fact that it will save him time—time to make other sales.

Car spraying

Did you read recently of an American survey indicating that the colour of cars had a bearing on the accident rate? It showed that cars finished in dark colours seemed more accident-prone than those in light colours. The safest colour was yellow. In the research sample of a thousand cars, yellow cars had fewer accidents than those in other colours. A garage-owner noticed this research and told one of his salesmen to canvass car-owners for orders for resprays. The salesman's approach was this:

"Good morning, Mr. Car Owner. It has recently been

proved that cars finished in yellow are much less accident-prone than cars in any other colour. I am from Garage Sprayers Ltd. and we can . . ."

He then explained that the owner's car could be resprayed in a golden yellow at a reasonable cost. Many orders resulted.

Advertising signs

This approach is made by a salesman of mobile window-display signs. He had learned from experience that if, at the approach stage, he mentioned the name of his company and what he was selling the reaction was generally negative. He therefore made this different approach:

"Good morning, Mr. Smith. I have been outside your shop for five minutes. During that time 74 people passed by. That is 888 an hour. Do you know that many more of them could be induced to stop and look in your window? I am from Window Displays Limited, and we have . . ."

It worked.

Petrol pumps

"Good morning, Mr. Garage Proprietor. Every day customers are lost by garages because motorists will not queue for petrol. They have to wait because assistants can only fill a tank at the speed of the pump. I want to tell you about a new pump which, when it is installed, does all the work for you. It will add up the cash, serve the petrol rapidly, save time. I am from the X Pump Company. . ."

Shirts to retailers

"Good morning, Mr. Hosier. It is a major expense, as you know, to send back faulty shirts to the manufacturers. At our factory, returns are negligible because of the great care we take in manufacture and testing. I am from the Best Shirt Company. . ."

Duplicators to offices

"Good morning, Mr. Office Manager. You can now have just one duplicator, not only for all office work but also to handle multiple runs and special systems which used to require very expensive printing machines. I am from. . ."

Fire prevention for shops and offices

"Good morning, Mr. Jones. Fire losses are now running at nearly £60 million a year. People like you don't want to have a share of that loss. I am from. . ."

Instant coffee to grocers

"Good morning, Mr. Brown. I have called especially to see you because nine out of ten grocers stock our products with great success because they have a quick turnover and leave a high margin of profit. As you are one of the few grocers who are not yet one of our satisfied customers, I want to prove to you what we can do for you. I am from . . ."

Frozen-food salesman to a grocer

"One of the difficulties of handling frozen foodstuffs is that the limited amount of storage space often restricts the variety you can handle. My company XYZ Ltd. have instituted a daily delivery scheme using insulated vans with every variety of frozen product . . ."

Cartons to manufacturers

"Mr. Smith, every day hundreds of cartons leave your factory for your customers throughout the country. Each carton could be a wonderful advertisement for you if it had a striking slogan in full colour. My company, XYZ Carton Co., have recently set up a design department to help our customers achieve first-class results with practically no extra cost involved."

Welding equipment to engineering companies

"Mr. Smith, you must obviously be interested in turning out the best welding job in the minimum time and with the least fatigue to your operators. My company, XYZ Ltd., manufacture what has been described by my customers as 'the fastest gun in the west' and I would like to tell you how it can help you . . ."

Caravans to private customers

"Because of the tremendous development in the sale of caravans, more and more owners are finding difficulty in locating a suitable site after they have bought their van. My company, XYZ Ltd., have made arrangements with site owners in many parts of the country to give priority to those people who buy their caravans from us . . ."

Scaffolding to builders

"Scaffolding equipment is usually required at short notice in the building trade, but only the larger builders can afford to buy adequate stocks. My company, XYZ Scaffolding Ltd., operate an extremely attractive rental scheme with depots strategically placed throughout the country to supply your needs within hours."

As an exercise, try and work out some factual approaches. You can do this by reading newspaper advertisements that contain selling facts about products or services. By working out approaches that could be used by other salesmen, you can more easily compose your own *factual approach*.

The question approach

The question approach is generally successful, for everyone likes answering questions.

If you are in a bus queue and someone asks the person next to you for direction to a post office, your ears prick up. If you know the way, you have the urge to interfere. You plan the route in your mind and you are disappointed if your neighbour knows the correct answer.

Haven't you always felt the urge to answer questions quickly on panel games? The television is switched on. A quiz programme is about to begin. The Chairman introduces the panel and explains that each member of the team will be asked questions and given points for correct answers. Father continues to read his paper as if he is not interested, mother goes on knitting, and daughter pretends she knows it all anyway. The Chairman asks the first question. Down goes father's paper. He knows the answer, and he can't get it out quickly enough. The second question is asked. Mother drops her knitting. "I know," she says. "I know, it's on the tip of my tongue." Daughter, still pretending to be unconcerned, is trying hard to get the correct answer before mother, father, and the members of the panel. Doesn't that happen to all of us when we are watching quiz programmes?

The question approach is based on the assumption that everyone likes to answer a question, especially if the subject interests them. So the question used at the approach by the salesman must relate to the buyer's business. Here are some examples:

Electric-light bulbs

A salesman representing a leading light-bulb manufacturer came to one of our courses. His company had just started to market the smaller-sized bulbs. The salesman told us that, although excellent sales followed the big advertising campaign, he encountered difficulties in opening new accounts with electrical dealers.

He explained that many retailers became argumentative. They insisted that their customers were used to the larger bulbs and would not be convinced that the smaller ones would give similar results. We suggested using this different approach:

"Good morning, Mr. Electrical Dealer. Would you

12

agree that your shelf-space is highly valuable to you?"
The retailer must answer: "Yes." "If, then," the salesman
continues, "you could display the same products and still
have 20% space available for other goods, you would
think it worth while, wouldn't you?" "Yes."

"Our new lamps are 20% smaller than those we used
to make. But they have the same output and last just as
long. You will not only find them quick-moving but, as
they take up so much less space on your shelves, you will
have more room to display more goods. I am from . . ."

Power drills

There are many manufacturers of power drills. It isn't
easy for a representative to think of a new approach, but
careful thought will always find a new angle. One salesman
of power drills found this:

"Good morning, Mr. Jones. Can you sell high-quality
power drills in your shop?"

This question prompted two thoughts in the prospect's mind.
First, this fellow doesn't think I can sell high-quality products;
I will show him I can. Second, he must be very certain of the
quality of his products to ask me that question. When he
answered "yes," the salesman continued:

"Then, sir, I can show you how you can make extra
profit by selling the most expensive but the finest quality
drill on the market. I am from . . ."

Treatments to a doctor

"Good morning, Dr. Brown. Isn't it true, doctor, that
more and more patients visit your surgery suffering from
migraine?"

"Yes, it is a growing 20th-century complaint."

"Well, sir, my company, XYZ Ltd., has developed a new
treatment about which an article appeared in the *Lancet*

recently, and I would like to amplify one or two of the points made in it."

Concentrated fertiliser to a farmer

"Good morning, Mr. Giles. Would you agree that one of the biggest overheads in farming today is that of labour costs?"

"Yes, I suppose so."

"Well, sir, my company, Better Fertilisers Ltd. has produced a new fertiliser which is so concentrated that much less labour is needed to spread it, but it is more effective than the normal type of fertiliser."

Paper tissues to a chemist

"Good morning, Mr. Brown. Do you agree that your job as a retailer is made much easier by manufacturers who go all out to stimulate public demand for their products?"

"Yes, that is so."

"My company, Tissues Ltd., conducts the biggest advertising campaign in the trade, and I would like to give you details of our new programme for the next three months."

Men's toiletries to a chemist

"Good morning, Mr. Smith. Isn't it your experience that a very large proportion of men's toiletries are purchased by women?"

"Yes, that is true."

"It is because of this that my company, XYZ Ltd., have designed their products for men but with women in mind. Let me show you an example of the new type of pack we have produced."

Paint to an architect

"Good morning, Mr. Smith. Isn't it true that today more of your clients are colour-conscious than ever before?"

"Yes."

"Because of this great awareness of colour schemes generally, my company, XYZ Ltd., has set up a new advisory department especially equipped to help you with background advice."

Insurance to a householder

"Good evening, Mrs. Jones. I understand from the local house agents that you have only recently bought and moved into this lovely house?"

"Yes, we have."

"The reason for my call is that most people in your position like to make quite sure that, should anything happen to the breadwinner, the house would not be forfeited to the building society. My company, Good Insurance Ltd., has an excellent scheme to cover this contingency and I would like to give you details of it."

The question approach can constantly be used with slight variations.

The reference approach

Products manufactured by Tack Industries Limited are sold throughout the world. Probably the most vital job of our export division is to find the right foreign concessionaire. Before appointing him, we insist that he sets up a sales organisation on similar lines to ours in Great Britain. The concessionaire must be willing to train salesmen, provide a sales manual, issue regular sales bulletins, and so on.

Many companies express eagerness to comply with these demands to obtain the concession but we know from long experience that they are not always capable of keeping their promises. We set about finding the right concessionaire by advertising in the appropriate country, and we get many replies. Each one is carefully vetted. But the search for the right company can resemble looking for a needle in a haystack.

Sometimes, an associate or a friend will recommend some-one to us. Then we are confident that we are off to a good start. The associate will know exactly what we require and would not recommend anyone who did not measure up to our standards.

Sometimes we receive a letter that begins:

"Our mutual friend, Mr. Brown, has suggested that we write to you to negotiate for the selling rights of your products in our country."

It isn't long before one of our executives is flying to see the writer of that letter. We know there will be a basis for dis-cussion.

The reference approach, in fact, is an immediate con-fidence-builder. Properly used, it will get attention for the salesman.

The reference approach builds immediate goodwill; here are some examples:

Packaging salesman

"Good morning, Mr. Brown. Recently we were able to make drastic reductions in packaging costs for White and Jones. Mr. White tells me he is an old friend of yours. We save him about £200 a month, and I feel sure we could help you in the same way . . ."

Wines and spirits salesman

"Good morning, Mr. Jones. Your friend, Mr. Brown of Brown and Wright, suggested that I should call to see you. He believes that our unique delivery service has helped to give better service to his customers and has also enabled him to keep his stock down. I am from . . ."

Knitwear salesman

"Good morning, Mrs. White. Would you please look at this letter? It has been written by the buyer of Brown's of Burston. She had a special display of our knitwear last month and was so pleased with the result that she wrote us this letter. You have a similar high-class establishment and..."

Juke-box salesman

"Good morning, Mr. Smith. I have come especially to see you at the suggestion of Mr. Williamson who runs the Bar-B-Q Restaurant on the other side of town. I believe, sir, he is a friend of yours. My company, XYZ Ltd., installed one of our juke-boxes in his premises some time ago and..."

Space salesman

"Good morning, Mr. Smith. My company, XYZ Publications Ltd. has specialised recently in advertising hotel facilities in selected areas. Our clients have been pleased with the results, and we are now extending the scope of our advertising. Your friend, Mr. White of the Imperial Hotel, Johnsonville, has used our magazine and was sure that you would be interested in the services we can offer you."

Here are some rules for using the reference approach:

1. Don't refer to a local rival who has sold your products well. This will be more likely to antagonise the prospect than to please him. Refer to someone a long way off who is not a competitor but in the same line of business.

2. Avoid such sentences as "Smith's of Birmingham sell these like hot cakes"; or "Whites of Whitley Bay sell thousands of them." The buyer who cannot buy in such large quantities may reply: "I am not interested in what other people do."

But wisely used, the reference approach is very strong.

The call-back approach

When a salesman calls regularly on customers, he should vary the approach, and dispense with stock phrases like:

"How are you?"
"Has the stock been moving?"
"Is trade any better?"
"Were the goods delivered on time?"
"Did the display arrive?"
"Anything for me today?"

These are time-wasters. No matter how frequently a salesman sees a customer, he can find something new to say about his products each time. Before each visit he should decide on a factual sentence, or a question, or a term of reference that will put fresh life into the sale. For example:

"Good morning, Mr. Jones. When I was here last month, I told you about our new advertising campaign. I have some facts for you now which should help you to decide on your stock requirements."

"Good morning, Mr. Smith. Have you noticed that over the past five weeks there has been a sudden demand for reds and greens? We have added some variations of these colours to our range."

"Good morning, Mr. White. Have you ever seen a better display than this one? It almost lines up exactly with what you suggested some months ago."

"Mr. Brown, after I left you last time I thought of an idea which would help you to sell more of . . ."

"Good morning, Mr. Green. I must apologise to you. When I was here five weeks ago, I didn't really explain in detail what a tie-up with our promotional campaign means, but you will remember you were very busy at the time. Do forgive me, but this is how it can help you . . ."

The order-takers use hackneyed approaches. The professional salesman thinks of something new at every call.

Other approaches

Most salesmen use the factual, question, or reference approach. These additional approaches can be used occasionally:

The curiosity approach

"Good morning, Mr. Smith. Have you ever seen a metal plate like this before? It can save you a lot of money. It is an accessory used in our new addressing machine . . ."

The fear approach

"Mr. Jones, what would happen to your house if a fire broke out while you and your children were asleep in bed? Our fire alarm . . ."

The gift approach

"Mrs. Smith? Good morning. Will you please accept this cleaning powder with our compliments? We want you to try it. I also want to show you . . ."

The personal interest approach

"Good morning, Mr. Jones. I was very interested to read your excellent letter in this morning's *Graphic*. Every statement you made was quite right, but naturally I was sorry to hear of the bad service you had received from the X Car Company. This need never happen to you again. I am from ABC Garages. We are sole distributors in the area for Y cars and I have called to ask you to let us show you a model of . . ."

You must assess the right approach for your product or service. But here are some you should never use:

"Good morning, Mr. Jones. It's very cold, isn't it?"

"Good morning, Mr. Smith. I have never seen such rain!"

"Good morning, Mr. Brown. What wonderful weather we are having!"

Your customers know what the weather is like without your telling them. Make the right approach and you are well on the way to a sale.

CHAPTER XI

CREATION OF CONFIDENCE

Someone may say of his doctor: "I have no confidence in him." It seems a ridiculous criticism. That doctor spent years of study and application for a degree. He dismembered frogs, helped to bring many babies into the world, assisted in major operations. Then he fixed his plate to the door, with the letters 'M.D.' after his name. He had similar knowledge and skills to other doctors.

If he is uncertain of a diagnosis, he can get advice from a consultant. He gets daily details of research carried out by large pharmaceutical organisations. But someone has no confidence in him. Why should this be?

The reason may be his manner, or his approach to the patient. He may be dogmatic, jumping to quick conclusions, and so the patient feels that he hasn't studied the case carefully. He may dither and have a brow of many furrows as he makes his diagnosis. He may mutter that it could be this or it could be that and the patient expects the worst.

We all lack confidence in a doctor who either doesn't appear very interested in us or seems to lack confidence in himself.

Delete the word 'doctor' from that paragraph and substitute 'salesman'.

It is only a short step from "I have no confidence in him" to "I don't trust him." Most of us have taken this view of someone's integrity. Maybe he was too glib, too smart, or too insistent in his desire to help us.

Or someone may say: "There's something about him that I don't like!" He may be shifty-eyed, oily in his manner, overwhelming in his flattery.

We have all remarked: "I wouldn't trust him any further

than I could throw him!" Meaning that he is too clever, hinting at his adroitness in outwitting one or deceiving another.

Judging by appearances

Our judgement of our fellows is often faulty. The salesman who appears too glib may be honest and trustworthy but cannot control his tongue. The shifty-eyed man may be nervous and disinclined to look straight ahead. The flatterer may be merely a fool. The salesman who boasts of his cleverness may be upright, but mistakenly believe that a show of brilliance impresses others.

The salesman must create confidence, but he often arouses mistrust from the moment he makes his approach. He must observe certain rules for building confidence.

He must have confidence in his products. A salesman is not a confidence-trickster. He must create an agreeable feeling between himself and his customers. Knowing that his goods will benefit the buyer, he will have no reservations about doing everything possible to obtain an order.

He must create confidence by his voice and his language. He must not exaggerate, or make claims that cannot be substantiated.

He must create confidence by his enthusiasm.

He must create confidence by the care with which he handles sales-aids.

He must create confidence by the judicious use of testimonial letters, advertising displays, and verbal-proof stories.

He must create confidence by his knowledge of his customer's business.

He must create confidence by his willingness to listen to his customer's problems.

The small company

The salesman joining a newly-formed or small company will soon appreciate the need for confidence-builders. Prospects may show lack of confidence in him and the company by saying: "I have never heard of you," or "How long have you been going?" or "I am not opening any more new accounts." To overcome these objections, the salesman's presentation must include a confidence-builder. He may well develop sentences like:

> "Our company has been established only about twelve months, but our managing director was for 20 years chief engineer with the largest electronics firm in America. It is his vast experience that has developed . . ."

> "We are only a small company, Mr. Brown, but we are local. That means that you will get prompt and personal service, not only from me but also from our managing director."

> "Because we are fairly small, we operate only in a limited area. This keeps our costs down and we can pass the benefit on to you."

The larger company

Sales managers or representatives with a large organisation believe that the good reputation of their company ensures the confidence of its customers for ever. This might be true if there were no competitors. But businesses large and small always have competitors.

Good salesmen may not attack their opponents' products directly, but they do so all the time indirectly.

A well-known fertiliser company was perturbed because sales in some areas were falling. An investigation showed that business was lost by weaker representatives to salesmen of smaller companies. They made no direct criticism of the larger organisation, but they inferred that better service could be given by a small, dynamically led company. The lesson was quickly learned by the large group, and every salesman was told to use a confidence-builder at every call.

This kind of sentence can be a confidence-builder for well-established companies:

"We spend nearly three-quarters of a million a year on research, and you receive the benefit. Of course, the time will come when smaller companies will copy us, but by then we will be even further ahead."

"There is no special merit in being large, but we have grown so rapidly because we are efficient. We always strive to improve service for our customers, and we will even give it at a loss if necessary." (The inference here is that a smaller company could not afford these losses.)

"Because of our wide ramifications, Mr. Brown, we can offer you a free survey. Our experts will come down here, take samples of your soil, and . . ."

Every salesman criticises competitors' products indirectly and so every salesman must build confidence to refute the implied criticism.

CONFIDENCE LOSERS

To build confidence, work out a selling sentence to be incorporated in the sales presentation. But first examine some confidence-losers.

Making exaggerated claims

When a salesman makes an exaggerated claim, confidence is lost. If, for example, the circulation of a magazine is 13,000 a month and a salesman tells a media buyer of an advertising agency that 30,000 copies a month are sold, confidence is lost. The buyer knows that, if such a circulation were true, a magazine would have its accounts audited and receive a certificate from the Audit Bureau of Circulations. If 14,000 were claimed, this might not be untrue, for circulation can fluctuate. But the 30,000 figure is a blatant lie, although no space-salesman claiming it believes that he is lying. It is, to him, an exaggeration.

If a salesman claims that there is practically no wear-and-tear with his product when a buyer, who may be a highly-qualified engineer, knows that there must be wear-and-tear, confidence is lost. If a salesman of a standard unit heater incorporating a fan tells a works engineer that the unit will heat in the winter and cool in the summer, confidence is lost. The engineer would know that only refrigeration would take the heat out of the air and so cool the atmosphere. A fan circulating air will have a cooling effect, but will not reduce the temperature of a room.

The foolish salesman exaggerates because he does not realise that the truth is much more likely to get him the order.

Attacking competitors

Although salesmen are always attacking each other in-directly—and this is fair enough—a direct attack on a competitor undermines the confidence of the buyer in the representative making it.

Foolish statements

A foolish statement, not necessarily an exaggeration, is a certain confidence-loser. For example, a salesman representing a very small company may talk wildly of his company's world-wide reputation. A typewriter salesman called on me some time ago and told me that his electric typewriter needed hardly any service. He may have believed this statement—but I didn't. Foolish statements can be made about delivery, advertising, or after-sales service. Only foolish salesmen make foolish statements that lose confidence.

Not keeping promises

The quickest way for a salesman to lose a customer's confidence is to make a promise he cannot keep. Typical is the speciality salesman, working on a commission basis, who tells a customer that he will call back soon after delivery to make certain that the equipment is correctly installed. When the equipment is installed, the salesman is usually much too busy trying to earn more commission from new prospects to call back.

Another example is the salesman calling on retailers who implies that he is giving sole rights to a particular product or range of goods. Because he is the only salesman working that territory, he may believe he can keep that promise. But there is nothing to stop other retailers sending an order direct to his company and getting delivery.

Once a salesman has broken a promise, confidence is lost for good.

Personal relations

Confidence is lost when a salesman attempts to be too friendly with a customer. Some salesmen are too ready with Christian names. Confidence is also lost if a salesman forgets the name of a prospect or customer.

CONFIDENCE-BUILDERS

A good appearance

At the risk of your exclaiming "Oh no! Not again!" I repeat the injunction that every salesman must have a good appearance. Repetition is essential to good teaching, so I make no apologies for it here. How can a customer believe that a company is prosperous and produces first-class goods when its representative resembles one of life's failures?

Background of company

Although a customer may have dealt with a salesman for many years, he must still be constantly reminded of the main reasons for the company's high reputation. Here are some sentences that project the right image of a company:

"Did you read in the Drapers' Record of the new machines we have just installed to give a much better finish to man-made fibres?"

"You have probably seen the photograph of our Managing Director in the papers recently. You might like to know that on his desk is a card with these words: 'Service to our customers must always have top priority.' Busy as he is, he sees all representatives and always wants to know from them if their customers are being well looked after."

"May I arrange for you to visit our factory? It is one of the most up-to-date production units in the country and it would help you to impress upon your customers the value they are buying when they buy our branded goods."

"Our company is 60 years old this month, but I know you will agree that it is very young in its outlook, always trying for better quality, better value."

Whether a company is large or small, there is always some aspect of its background which can be turned into a confidence-builder.

Satisfied users

The reference approach is itself a confidence-builder. But often you will keep testimonial letters to build confidence later in the sale. The prospect will not read one line by line. If you hand it to him, he won't read it at all. If you hold the letter, he will glance through it. A better course is to hold the letter and read it through with the prospect, but even this may waste time if the letter is long. Best of all, mark those parts of the letter with most interest for customers and prospects. When you produce it, say something like:

"Here is a letter from Browns', who have been so successful with our products. This part will interest you . . ."

Then read the few lines that you wish to register with him.

More confidence-builders

Confidence can be built by providing records, reports, results from advertising campaigns, guarantees, seals of approval, newspaper cuttings, copies of D.M.A. letters and promotional schemes.

Build confidence at every call.

CHAPTER XII

SELLING THE PRODUCT

Just imagine for a moment that you are at home one evening with your wife. You have been married three years. You are both in a very happy mood. Why? Because your chief has just told you that he is giving you a rise of £x a week.

You and your wife are discussing what you should do with this unexpected windfall. There are so many claims on the money. You consider saving it in order to have the house repainted. You tinker with the idea of a glorious holiday abroad. Above all, however, you both want a car.

Soon you will be inspecting the cars-for-sale advertisements. You have the deposit already, put by for a rainy day, and the extra income will meet the monthly repayments on either a new "mini" or a streamlined coupé a few years old.

Then, interrupting the atmosphere of excitement and anticipation, comes a sharp knock at the front door. Hoping that it is your friend William, who has a car and has never stopped telling you that you ought to get one, you open the door.

It is a stranger. "Good evening, Mr. Brown," he says. "Mrs. Brown asked me to call this evening as she felt that I could help both of you."

The stranger is an insurance salesman, whom your wife had seen earlier that day and told to call back.

"I'm very busy just now," you mumble.

"I'm so sorry to intrude," he replies, "but what I have to say won't take long, and you and your wife may count it as the best half-hour you have ever spent."

Reluctantly you ask him in. You hardly listen to him at first. Your thoughts are on that car. Then he starts to explain the benefits of insurance. You break in to tell him that you want to delay matters, as you intend to buy a car. The salesman's reply shocks you.

"I can see," he says "that you are a very happy couple, and you want to show your affection for your wife by buying this car. But what would happen if that was all you were able to leave her?"

You sit bolt upright. Your wife pales.

"Forgive me for being so frank," says the salesman, "but if you were to die, how would your wife manage?"

The salesman has understood that only a shock will give you a truer perspective. You are unsettled, and the salesman goes on: "The car is not a great asset. There might be further payments to be made if your wife wanted to keep it. Could she find this money without your income? The policy I suggest for you will give you a nest-egg later in life. But, more important, it is a safeguard for your wife if ever she should be widowed."

He may then add that most city editors of newspapers advise the small investor only to buy equities when he has cash to spare. First, they insist, buy saving certificates, then perhaps a few premium bonds, and later make a small investment in a well-established building society. Only when the small investor still has cash to spare, should he buy equities.

"You are surely in the same position," says the salesman, "although you do not deal in stocks and shares. Ensure security for yourself and your wife before getting a car. An insurance policy will bring you peace of mind—and what is more important than that?"

The odds are on your taking out that policy, and postponing the car until you have another rise. You always *needed* the insurance. You knew you should think of the future. When, however, there is a choice between a *need* and a *want*, most of us will settle for the *want*. If that insurance salesman had not called, you would have bought the car.

If he had called and been a poor salesman, you would still have had the car. He turned your *need* for the insurance into a *want*; then he made you *want* the insurance more than the car.

The professional salesman is a '*want-maker*'. His strong presentation makes prospects want his product or service.

How does he do this? How can you become a '*want-maker*'? By selling benefits, benefits and still more benefits. When benefits of the insurance policy exceeded the benefits of a car, the insurance salesman knew that he had found another policy-holder.

Building benefits

Benefits are built around facts. Benefits are obtained by research. They are found more easily when buying motives are understood. Why do people buy? For the benefits they receive? Yes, but what kind of benefits interest them? Psychologists have written at length about buying motivation. The subconscious mind has been probed, subliminal thinking has been exposed. Whether the psychologists are right or wrong, more than forty years of selling have proved to me that there is nothing complicated about buying motives. Some people always look for the difficulties in any problem, although the solution may be quite simple. There are established motives for buying. If we link our sales presentation to them, we cannot go wrong.

The main buying reasons are:

gain of money;
satisfaction of caution;
satisfaction of pride;
utility value;
sentimental reasons;
pleasure;
to benefit health;
to satisfy hunger;

envy;
love;
fear;
to obtain security;
to obtain more leisure;
to gain a feeling of importance.

Here are some applications of these buying reasons to various products:

Gain of money

The retailer buys merchandise to resell at a profit; the manufacturer buys component parts to make a product to sell at a profit. When a buyer is allowed extra discounts, and so switches from his previous supplier, he is motivated by gain of money. There is gain of money when it is saved. If a salesman can prove that a washing-machine will cost less than the total laundry bills over a period—he is using gain of money to sell.

Satisfaction of caution

Car safety-belts are sold to cautious motorists. All kinds of safety devices that protect employees are sold to works directors. To satisfy caution, companies install burglar and fire alarms.

Satisfaction of pride

One reason for buying a car may be pride of ownership. Pride is satisfied when clothes are bought for children, or an electric hedge-cutter helps to produce the smartest hedge in town. A good letter-heading can satisfy pride. A man may be proud to own a golf-club similar to one used by an open champion. A retailer may feel proud of his new shop-front, a director proud of his newly-equipped office, a secretary proud of her electric typewriter.

Utility value

Many products are chiefly bought for the services they give. A vacuum-cleaner may save time and effort, but the main buying reason is that it collects dust, grit, and dirt quickly. A salesman may dislike driving and have no pride in his car; he may be only too pleased to leave it in his garage at weekends. He uses it during the week for its utility value.

Sentimental reasons

A painting, a piece of jewellery, or furniture may be bought for sentimental reasons.

For pleasure

A perfect piece of machinery can give pleasure to an engineer. Cigars give the pleasure of after-dinner smoking. Pleasure comes from buying gifts for others, or a new tie for ourselves. Because a calendar gives pleasure, manufacturers will reproduce well-known paintings on them, or pay artists high fees for original nudes or landscapes.

To benefit health

This takes in heating, ventilating, and lighting equipment. A well-made chair can benefit a typist's health. A string vest can be healthier for the outdoor man. Health, too, can benefit from the use of disinfectants, sporting equipment, cleaning services, and pharmaceuticals.

To satisfy hunger

This applies to all edibles sold to caterers, restaurants, or hoteliers.

Envy

No one likes to believe that he would buy something through envy, but many retailers have added to their stock because they envy the display of a competitor.

Minks and diamonds can be sold through this motive.

Consultancy services and advertising can be sold because a managing director envies the prosperity of a competitor.

Love

Gifts are bought out of love. Encyclopaedias are acquired through love for children; domestic appliances are sometimes bought through affection; books are bought through love of good writing.

Fear

Many retailers decided to be the first in the district to use trading stamps, for fear that a rival might beat them to it. Insurance policies and fire-fighting equipment may be bought through fear of the future. A new shop-front might be installed by a retailer fearful of creating an old-fashioned image. Deodorants are sold because people's fear of having body odours.

To obtain security

Safes and locks give security. Security services are used for the same reason. Parents will give private education to their children for security later in life.

To obtain more leisure

This is a reason for buying domestic appliances, self-service counters, dictating machines, and so on.

To gain a feeling of importance

A large house can give a man importance. So can a Savile Row suit. The installation of a computer can add to a managing director's self-importance. Sole distributing rights make a retailer important.

Men crave attention, and a selling sentence that stresses their importance is a strong benefit.

Your product—Your service

List every benefit by checking every buying reason against your product or service. It is improbable that a salesman can use all fourteen reasons, but the more he has, the stronger his sales presentation will be.

How does this apply to two very different products?

A Computer

Gain of Money	Yes	Profits will increase with greater efficiency.
Satisfaction of Caution	Yes	Human errors will be eliminated.
Satisfaction of Pride	Yes	A computer is a symbol of a forward-looking managing director.
Utility Value	Yes	It will automatically provide all data required.
Sentimental Reasons	No	—
For Pleasure	Yes	It will please those who operate it.
Benefit to Health	Yes	It will cut down the strain and worry of decisions made on false evidence.
To Satisfy Hunger	No	—
Envy	Yes	Competitors may already use similar equipment.
Love	No	—
Fear	Yes	Fear of what will happen in the future if the managing director does not buy a computer.
To Obtain Security	Possibly	It depends on the business.
To Obtain Leisure	Yes	Problems can be solved in half the time. Working late to provide figures as a basis for decisions is avoided.

To Give A Feeling of
    Importance   Yes   —

The Sales manager of a company manufacturing computers should study such a list and work out the benefits of his computer. This is the basis of a sales story for his representatives.

A Tennis Racket Sold To Retailers

Gain of Money	Yes	The racket is well-known and will have a quick turnover and increase sales. There will be extra discounts for larger quantities.
Satisfaction of Caution	Yes	With Great Britain doing well in the Davis Cup, there could be a bigger demand for these rackets.
Satisfaction of Pride	Yes	The retailer will display the best rackets in the world.
Utility Value	Yes	The splendid balance of the racket, the care with which it is manufactured, help the retailers' customers to improve their tennis.
Sentimental Reasons	No	—
For Pleasure	Yes	A retailer will be pleased with the special display provided by the manufacturer, and with his participation in a national advertising campaign.

Benefits to health, satisfaction of hunger, envy, or love, are largely inappropriate.

Fear	Yes	If the retailer does not carry good stocks, he may not meet the demands in the summer.

To Obtain Security	Yes	If he does not stock the racket, he may lose business to competitors. Once a customer has gone to a competitor he may not return.
To Obtain More Leisure	No	—
To Give A Feeling of Importance	Yes	He may have the sole rights for the racket in this area.

Other benefits may derive from the special gut used, the Newflo frame, the design perfected after years of research, a leading player's autograph, or from similar rackets being used by international champions.

WHICH MEANS THAT . . .

Listing benefits and giving them in quick succession is not salesmanship. No one is interested in facts he may not grasp. Here are some that a salesman of heavy-duty tyres might give to the owner of a fleet of lorries:

Give excellent service;
Cool-running nylon is used;
Special wear-resisting rubber-plus treads are incorporated;
Stronglife compound resists abrasion;
Tyres are tested over thousands of miles of road;
Special toughened side walls resist blow-outs;
They cost the same as ordinary tyres.

All these are valuable benefits, but how would a buyer react to the salesman's claim that "cool-running nylon is used"?

Does every lorry-owner know about cool-running nylon? In addition to listing the main selling features, they must be presented as readily understood customer benefits. Many salesmen think that all buyers know the intricacies and technical refinements of their goods. It is not true. A housewife knows nothing about a totally enclosed motor. The chief engineer may not have up-to-date knowledge of a newly-developed steel ball and rod charge; the retailer may not know the difference between a fashioned garment and one of circular knit. Buyers must understand every benefit, and the salesman helps them to do so by remembering three words:

which means that

They are constant reminders that the salesman should explain benefits in terms of the buyer's interest.

Revert again to the selling of tyres. Use the same benefits, but with the 'which means that' technique.

"They give maximum service, *which means that* your lorry-drivers concentrate on getting from place to place quickly without having to worry about tyre trouble . . ."

"Cool-running nylon is used, *which means that* the temperature is kept down between road surface and tyre. You get more miles from each set of tyres, because heat causes wear and tear. The shape of the tyre is maintained, which means smoother running and lower petrol consumption . . ."

"We use special wear-resisting rubber-plus treads, *which means that* your drivers will travel in safety when roads are icy and deliver their goods on time . . ."

"A stronglife compound is used to resist abrasion, *which means that* you will get more wear from the tyres even when a lorry is driven over miles of rough roads . . ."

"The tyres have been tested on thousands of miles of roads, *which means that* we solve your problems before you encounter them . . ."

"Toughened side walls will resist blow-outs, *which means that* your drivers can maintain the highest possible speeds without fear, and that means better service to your customers . . ."

"They cost the same as ordinary tyres, *which means that*

you pay no extra for this long-life, economical, safe tyre . . ."

Here are many instances from some of the varied companies that use this Tack formula:

Sketchley Ltd.—Sketchley Overall Service

"Ours is an overall service, *which means that* we take over all the problems of having stocks of the right size and type to satisfy you and your employees."

Rest Assured Ltd.—Mattresses

"We put a cushioning of fleece or woollen-mixture felt on the winter side of our mattresses, and white cotton felt on the other, *which means that* the bed keeps warmer on the winter side."

F. S. Stowell Ltd.—Wine Merchants

"Here is a 1959, one of the finest claret vintages of the century. Current list prices are extremely low, *which means that* if you buy now there will be no shortage for you and your friends when the wine comes to its peak."

Q. V. F. Limited—Chemical Engineers in Glass

"These units produce technically pure products and are constructed in glass, *which means that* you can *see* this . . ."

Aladdin Industries Limited—Oil Heaters

"One gallon of paraffin contains 160,000 British Thermal Units, equal to 47 units of electricity, *which means that* the heat produced by this gallon of paraffin, for 2s. 4d. in an Aladdin oil-heater would cost 5/- from an electric fire . . ."

Crusader Insurance Co. Ltd.

"We sell a plan for retirement, *which means that* complete security in your old age is assured."

Pinchin Johnson & Associates Ltd.—Decorative Paint Division

"This aluminium paint incorporates highly-polished

leafing aluminium in a silicone medium and will be un-affected by heats of up to 1000°F, *which means that* if this material is used on your exhaust stacks their appearance will be maintained for a much longer time than with conventional paints."

Spillers Limited—Animal Feed

"Our Calf Cudlets have been designed to replace a whole milk diet via early weaning, *which means that* the calf can be reared more cheaply, with less labour and with reduced incidence of nutritional upset."

L. M. Van Moppes & Sons (Diamond Tools) Ltd.

"This is a new design in diamond wheel dressing tools. Its purchase price is much in line with ordinary price dressers. It is however, intended to be used to destruction without the necessity of resetting, *which means that* fewer tools need to be stocked to cover the resetting time, and also the machine operator spends less time changing his diamond."

Drake & Fletcher Ltd.—Engineers

"The centrifugal fan used only on Victair sprayers is far quieter than all competitive types of sprayer, *which means that* there is far less fatigue for the operator."

F. M. S. (Farm Products) Ltd.

"These Carrot Fingers come to you in an attractive polythene-lined carton and are already cleaned, peeled and cut, *which means that* you save time and money on preparation and labour, because all you have to do is add boiling water and cook in the normal way."

Yardley & Co. Ltd.—Perfumers and Fine Soap Makers

"You will see that our talcum powder is packed in a new plastic container. It is light and easy to handle, unbreakable and rust proof, *which means that* the true fragrance of the talc is preserved for much longer than if any other form of packaging were used."

Blick Time Recorders Limited

"This is a Blick fully-automatic, one-hand-operated, electric card-system time-recorder, printing lateness and overtime in red for rapid analysis in your accounts department, *which means that* there is no time wasted. Staff clock in and out without delays or fumbling; they just put the card in the machine, and the rest is automatic."

Ferranti Ltd.—Electrical and General Engineers

"We cut the core iron plates to have mitred joints so accurate that the flux path has a minimum distortion, *which means that* your running costs for iron losses will be reduced to a minimum."

I. & R. Morley Ltd.—Hosiery Manufacturers

"This underwear is made from fabric knitted in such a way that it produces efficient insulating properties, *which means that* the garment is suitable for both summer and winter."

Slazengers Limited—Sports Goods Manufacturers

"In the old days tennis balls started smooth and wore even smoother, so that control in play was much more difficult. The Slazenger Tennis ball is covered with a specially developed cloth called T.W. or tennis weave—a combination of wool and nylon—*which means that* it will wear in new-ball condition for hours of play."

Chloride Batteries Limited

"This Auto-fil battery can be accurately topped up in 30 seconds, *which means that* the men on your forecourt spend much less time on free service." (The benefit is the reduced cost of forecourt service.)

Lansing Bagnall Ltd.—Fork Trucks and Towtractor Manufacturers

"With this truck you will reduce your gangways to 6

feet, *which means that* you will store 20% more material in this warehouse."

Price

After the sales presentation, the sale must now move smoothly to the close. But a buyer will need to know the price of a product or service before he is prepared to sign the order.

Speciality salesmen are taught to conceal the price as long as possible. They use such sentences as:

"I shall come to that in a moment, Mr. Brown . . ."

"I can't tell you until I know your exact requirements."

"Price is not important, because our service will make you a profit."

"You may want three, or six. After I have made a survey, I can give you the exact price. At this stage, it could only be a guess."

The longer a salesman withholds the price, provided he stresses benefits all the time, the more likely he is to complete the sale. If a price is given too quickly, the prospect may decide that it is too high on insufficient evidence. But when a customer demands a price and clearly shows he will not be fobbed off, then it must be given.

There are four rules for this:

1. By means of his prepared sales sequence, the representative should explain all the benefits he can before he gives the price.

2. When a price is quoted in the middle of the sale, he should pursue his sales story without pause. He should not wait for the buyer's comment.

3. When possible, preface the price with the word 'only'.

4. A salesman should not be afraid of the price, but must always justify it.

Benefits outweigh Price.

Benefits create Sales.

CHAPTER XIII

CLOSING THE ORDER

Archie Compston was one of the great golf instructors. For many years he was professional at the Coombe Hill Golf Club, Kingston, which had an important annual competition, a match-play championship. Once Archie was dourly surveying the 18th green. The final of the championship was being played, and the two contestants were all square after the 17th. Everything depended on the last hole. On the 18th green, Compston looked at two balls. One player was on in three and about 8 feet from the hole. The other player had taken four shots, and his ball was about 10 feet from the pin.

The odds favoured the player with the lesser score. The ball to be struck first was the one 10 feet away. It was cleanly hit and finished about two inches from the hole. The other player conceded the putt, and his adversary was down in six. Now it was his turn to putt. He lined up the ball carefully, and then struck it firmly—too firmly, for it rolled 4 feet past the hole. There was a gasp from the gallery, but Compston's face expressed nothing. The player was very upset and he took care with his next putt, which he had to sink to win. He was too careful, only half hit the ball, and left it 2 feet short. Now he was putting for a half, and was very tense. The silence was broken only by a flag fluttering from a mast. Once more the player who was favourite putted. The ball crept towards the hole, and he was transfixed. His caddy urged the ball to drop, but it didn't drop; it stayed on the lip of the hole. Four putts had been taken—and the favourite had lost.

Later, over a drink at the bar, the loser said to Archie Compston: "I can't get over it. I had three perfect shots to the green, and then I lost because of one bad putt—the first one that I hit too strongly."

Compston drank his beer, put his glass down, and said slowly: "That putt didn't lose you the game."

"What do you mean?" asked the player.

"Those shots to the green lost you the game," said Compston. "You didn't use your head."

"But", expostulated the player, "I hit the ball really well. I cleared the rough from the tee, got well into the fairway, the second wasn't far short of the green—what could be better than that?"

"What you should have done," said Compston, "was to have made sure of an uphill putt. Your pitch on to the green went too far, so you had to putt downhill."

"But that wasn't so easy," answered the player.

"Exactly," said Compston. "You are a natural hooker. Your shot from the tee, therefore, went to the left although the ball was well hit. That was because you went all out from the tee. You shouldn't have gone for distance, but tried to keep the ball on the right side of the fairway. It happened again with your second shot; it kept to the left. This happens to you nine times out of ten at the hole. You should have remembered that before you struck the ball. If you had used your head, you would have lost only a little distance and would have needed a longer iron to reach the green in three. But that wouldn't have mattered. You were on the left, so you had to clear a bunker that guarded the approach to the green. If you had been on the other side of the fairway, you need not have worried about that bunker. You had to hit your third shot fairly hard and firm to clear the bunker, and this sent your ball past the pin, leaving you with one of the worst putts in golf—downhill. Nine times out of ten, with a tense player dependent on a single putt, he will jab the ball instead of stroking it and it will run downhill past the hole. That's what you did. You didn't lose because of that putt; you lost when you were teeing up on the 18th. If you had thought ahead, you would have played each shot to keep right of the fairway and had an easy run into the pin. You didn't use your head."

How many times have professional golfers said to a player: "Use your head"? How many times have sales managers said to salesmen: "Use your head"?

The golf match was not lost because of that putt. It was lost because the player did not consider carefully the shots leading up to it. The golfer thought he was playing his shots well, but he wasn't. The salesman who fails to close a sale believes that he has sold well and blames his inability to close on some last-minute mishap. Sales, however, are not lost during the last moment of the sale, but during the sales presentation itself.

A salesman will insist: "I was doing so well but I just failed to clinch it." He was *not* doing well. He was kidding himself that his selling was brilliant.

The only certain way to close orders is to have a strong presentation. There is no better advice. But there are ways of nudging the buyer into signing the order after he has been convincingly sold. No method of closing a sale will succeed if the sales presentation has been weak.

A horse to the water

Over thirty years ago, I heard Paul Hervey, now managing director of that dynamic company, Hervey International Ltd., give a brilliant answer to a salesman who thought that orders were lost at the final stage of a sale.

The salesman had said: "Mr. Hervey, I know I sell well. I can take them right up to the water, but I can't make 'em drink!"

Paul Hervey replied: "It is not your job to make them drink. You have to make them *thirsty*."

The salesman must make the prospect so thirsty that he will drink of his own accord. The prospect must sell himself on a proposition. Then he is not *made* to buy; he will *want* to buy.

14

No psychological moments

It was once believed that there was one psychological moment to close a sale and, if it was missed, so was the order. I remember a salesman telling me:

"You've got to get them to the boil, and, if you let them off the boil, you've lost the order. You can never warm them up again."

Since then thinking has drastically changed. No one believes in the solitary psychological moment for closing an order. It is closed by taking the prospect through a sales sequence step by step until the logical completion.

Buying signals

The psychological moment, salesmen once said, is indicated by a buying signal. Some word, movement, or gesture by the prospect shows his readiness to buy.

In theory this may be true; in practice it doesn't always work. Many salesmen who close an order when a buyer shows interest in one aspect of a proposition have found that the order is subsequently cancelled. If a sale is closed too quickly this can easily happen. The buyer may be swayed by the personality of the salesman, but has second thoughts afterwards. Some of his doubts will not have been answered. He may change his mind and cancel the order. Here are rules for timing the close:

1. When a prospect has been given the complete presentation and he clearly understands it, the order must be closed.
2. Do not give an entire presentation before closing the order when the prospect is anxious to buy. He may have been completely sold on the product or service by advertising, by having seen it at an exhibition stand, or by having been introduced to it by another salesman. He was merely waiting for a representative to call in order to place an order.

3. With consumer goods, you cannot tell a complete story about each line unless only one or two are carried. A salesman with a wide range of products must make several closes. As he shows each line, he must try for an immediate decision. He then makes an entry on his order form. He repeats the procedure until he builds up the whole order for every product.

After the presentation, a buyer usually indicates his readiness to buy by giving a buying signal. The salesman can then close without more ado. If he talks after he has finished the presentation, he can easily talk himself out of the order. In the same way, at a film or play, we have all said at some time: "It went on too long."

We may have enjoyed the first hour-and-a-half but lost interest as the actors outstayed their welcome. Once the major part of the presentation is done and you are given a buying signal—close. Here are some buying signals:

The prospect's words

"Can you deliver fairly quickly?"
"Do these sell well in . . .?"
"Will it take up much room?"
"Will it help to . . .?"
"I have been thinking about this for some time."
"Have you any other colours?"
"What credit do you give?"
"Are you going to advertise it?"
"Are spare parts readily available?"

The prospect's actions

He studies the order form.
He re-reads part of a sales brochure.
He looks at the stock on the shelves.
He looks at the sample again.
He looks towards a place where the equipment could be installed.

His movements

He walks from his office into the factory or warehouse,
    where the salesman has suggested the equipment be
    installed.

He moves towards his shop-window to see whether it can
    accommodate a display.

He walks out of his shop to see where a sign could be
    fitted.

He takes a sample to show an assistant.

He nods his agreement.

Look for these buying signals. They will help you to close
the order smoothly and easily. You have made the prospect
'thirsty'.

Someone once said that a sale is made up of a lot of little
"yesses" which add up finally to one big "yes". This happens
exactly when the salesman obtains the buyer's agreement
to each step in his sales sequence. It isn't good enough to take
it on trust that a prospect agrees with you. He must show his
agreement by saying "yes" to each of your sales points. You
must obtain these "*yes*" responses.

If there are ten main benefits to be explained to, and
understood by, a buyer during a sales sequence, the salesman
must obtain a "yes" response to each one. If the response is
negative or non-committal, he must not continue with the
presentation. The prospect's mind must be cleared of any
misconception. When a salesman cannot close a sale despite
a good presentation, it is generally because of a negative
response to one of the buying reasons.

The prospect may not always be aware of the reason why
he cannot decide to buy. For example, a salesman may have
reached the step, 'creation of confidence'.

He may claim: "We are one of the largest manufacturers
in the country of steel-ended tangle bars."

The prospect may answer: "I have never seen your advertisements in the trade paper."

The salesman then replies: "Well, you are a very busy man, and can't see every advertisement. But I assure you that we do advertise regularly."

Thinking he has answered the buyer's query, the salesman goes on with his presentation. At the end, however, the prospect says he wants to think it over for a while. The salesman cannot understand the reason.

When the prospect showed that he had not heard of his company, the salesman should have produced evidence, copies of advertisements, or brochures illustrating factories or branches abroad. Only when he had allayed all doubts about his company's strength and stability, should he have added:

"Most firms are never as famous as they think they are, but you are quite clear about our company now aren't you, Mr. Brown?"

If Mr. Brown firmly answered "yes" the salesman could continue with the presentation.

Buying a car

I recently decided to buy a new car. A dealer arranged for a trial run. I soon realised that, when I depressed the brake pedal, it knocked against my left foot, which was resting against the automatic gear-box housing. The salesman stressed the comfort of the car. I told him that there did not appear to be enough room for the left foot to rest comfortably on the floor. He replied: "Oh, you will soon get used to that."

If he had noticed how I was manoeuvring my left foot, he would have seen that I was concerned at the lack of space. He went on to enthuse about the smoothness of the engine. The trial run ended. I did not buy.

That salesman may well have told his manager that I didn't buy because I could get a better price for my old car. This is the usual excuse for a car salesman who doesn't close a sale. But it did not apply to me.

I kept my old car for another year, and then arranged another trial run with a different distributor. The salesman again reached the sales step covering the comfort of the car. He told me how the seat could be adjusted to suit any driving position. It was then that I said: "Yes, it is a very comfortable seat, but the manufacturers have not given any more room for my left foot than in the last model. The pedal knocks against it when I brake."

The salesman said at once: "Will you stop the car for a moment, Mr. Tack."

I pulled up. He showed me that the carpet over the gear box was not properly fitted and so reduced the floor space. If I was not happy about it he said a smaller rubber pad could be fitted over the pedal. He suggested that I should rest my foot in another position, I did so, and found it comfortable. He then asked: "Are you quite happy now, Mr. Tack, about the floor space for your left foot?"

"Yes," I replied. And "Yes" I said later when he asked me for the order.

To close orders you must get "yes" responses throughout the presentation. Use the question-and-agreement technique in such ways as:

"You admit that this automatic switch must save you money?"

"Don't you agree that this display will be most effective?"

"You will enjoy the comfort, won't you?"

"It will fit into that space quite easily, won't it?"

"You would like to have an odour-free atmosphere, wouldn't you?"

"You prefer the better quality paper, don't you?"

"You do agree that your name on the carton is good advertising?"

"You do find the keys much quicker to the touch, don't you?"

It must be yes, yes, yes—all the way to the close.

Stickability

After I had given a talk on salesmanship that stressed the need for a salesman to have *stickability*, the managing director of a company manufacturing cardboard containers came up to me. As he approached, I recalled that he had once said: "I hate the idea of salesmanship. My men are representatives—not salesmen."

Wryly, I said to him: "I understand you have no great faith in person-to-person selling."

He smiled and answered: "Oh, I've come a long way since I made that rather fatuous remark about salesmen. I now agree wholeheartedly that no company can exist without person-to-person selling. But I'm afraid I cannot agree with you about stickability. This seems like high-pressure stuff to me—overdoing things, you know. Why should someone be pestered by a salesman when he has no intention of buying? If any salesman tried that on me, I'd throw him out."

After I had tried to put him right about high-pressure selling, the conversation went like this:

A.T. "Why do you employ salesmen?"

M.D. "To show my goods and interest customers in them."

A.T. "Not to sell them?"

M.D. "Of course they must also sell."

A.T. "Do they sell only to people who want to buy?"

M.D. "Unfortunately not. That's why I have to employ them."

A.T. "Then you agree that, to sell your goods, the salesmen must influence the mind of a customer?"

M.D. "Yes, I suppose so."

A.T. "Do you always buy because of a sudden impulse?"

M.D. "No, of course not."

A.T. "You want the full facts."

M.D. "Yes."

A.T. "If you are given the full facts, and you need a salesman's product, but still you decide not to buy, isn't it the duty of the salesman to convince you that you are wrong?"

M.D. "Yes, I suppose it is."

A.T. "What has happened is either that you are not clear about certain facts, or you want to examine competitors' prices before deciding."

M.D. "Well, that may be true."

A.T. "Do you want your salesmen to retire from a sale so that your competitors can take over?"

M.D. "Definitely not."

A.T. "That is what stickability means. If a salesman has faith in his product, he should exert himself to get an order at every interview. If he fails, the cause may be circumstances beyond his control, a bad presentation, or lack of stickability. You must agree with that."

M.D. "Well, yes, there is something in what you say. But I still don't like the sound of the word 'stickability'."

A.T. "We needn't argue over words. You may prefer persistence or determination. But let me give you final proof. We carried out research amongst a panel of buyers, and we learned from it that orders were frequently lost because the salesman left while a buyer was still deliberating the size of an order. Stickability means staying a little longer. The strong salesman always does that. The weak man gives up too quickly."

The managing director must have been convinced; he sent all his salesmen to one of our training courses.

Stickability does not mean talking long after the full presentation has been given. It does not mean boring the prospect. It means probing and asking questions to find why the buyer will not sign an order. Many buyers say "no" as a matter of course. A weak salesman takes the first "no" for an answer. He is easily put off by a request for literature, or a letter to be written, or a call to be made at another time. He clutches at these excuses, for he can still hope for an order one day.

A sale is closed most easily when a presentation is given in full and when there is a selling situation. In other words, the buyer must be in position to place an order. The speciality salesman knows that his best chance of completing a sale is at the first call; he can add nothing new to his presentation at subsequent visits. 80% of sales by speciality men are closed at the first call.

Representatives selling consumer goods must also close sales at each visit.

When lengthy negotiations must take place, and quotations and drawings submitted, no sale can be closed at a first call. The order, however, must be finalised as soon as there is a selling situation. It might be three months or a year after the first contact is made. But then, when the prospect has all the facts for a decision, the sale must be closed. This applies whether the order is for £100 or £100,000.

Many salesmen, asked to submit quotations, lose orders because they substitute the G.P.O. for themselves. A postman can merely deliver a quotation; a salesman can deliver and sell. One of Britain's top salesmen, selling engineering equipment, takes every quotation to a prospect personally. He opens the interview with:

"I have brought it to you personally so that we can go through it and make sure that we have met all your requirements."

Then he sells all over again, and, more often than not, he closes while his competitors are still writing letters and waiting for replies.

A most experienced salesman once gave me this advice:

"Keep seven coins in your left trouser pocket. At the first 'no' put one coin in the right pocket. Do the same for the second 'no'. Keep on selling; you will get most orders long before you have to move the seventh coin.

"But if you must move that coin, transfer it to the other pocket, pick up your hat—and leave. The buyer is a better salesman than you."

Stepping up the order

When closing a sale, a salesman should not accept a small order when he may get a larger one. Some salesmen are so grateful for small mercies that they are delighted with any order at all. Salesmen of capital goods can often sell extras after the main sale. Consumer-goods salesmen, while never overloading the retailer, must satisfy his full requirements. They must persist with the retailer so that he stocks every line they carry. They must strive to increase the size of the order by mentioning alternative colours or suggesting that extra sales can be achieved by stocking different sizes. Good salesmen think in terms of what the retailer can sell, not of what he should buy. If he is understocked and runs out of a line, he will lose those customers who buy elsewhere. The good salesman knows that in fairness to both his customer and his company, he must get the maximum order at every call. Salesmen are often so afraid of overselling the retailer that they undersell him; the goods are not displayed, stocks run out, and the field is wide open for a competitor.

Techniques for closing a sale

There are many closing techniques for getting the prospect's final decision when he doesn't buy without prompting.

The assumption close

Towards the end of the sale the representative assumes that an order will be placed and makes it obvious:

"You prefer to have the work carried out while you are on holiday, no doubt."

"When the stock is delivered, I will call back to help with the display."

"You can, if you wish, phone me personally for spare parts."

"I believe you like the red finish best, and I must say that I agree with you. It will be the red, then?"

"I will make a note of the best time and day for an engineer to call and fix the equipment, and I will confirm it to you in writing."

The salesman assumes; the buyer reacts; and the order is signed. The assumption close is, however, implicit throughout the sale. Whatever close a salesman uses, he should assume from the start that he will get the order and constantly refer to "*your* installation," "*your* deliveries," "*your* preferences."

The alternative close

A direct request for an order invites a direct answer. A salesman may sometimes say: "You have decided to buy then, Mr. Jones," or "You will place your order now, Mr. Brown, won't you?"

But the replies could be "yes"—or they could be "no". If "no", the salesman has the difficult job of making the prospect change his mind.

When a prospect hesitates, it is usually wrong to put a direct question to him. You lose little with the alternative close. By offering the prospect alternatives, you assume that he will buy and that his only decision concerns minor details. Here are some alternative closes:

"Would you prefer the unit to be finished in black or grey?"

"Will you have a gross, or two gross?"

"We can install the equipment by the door leading into the factory, or beneath the windows. Which do you prefer?"

Few products or services do not lend themselves to this form of closing. Salesmen of advertising space can say:

"Will you take advantage of our discount for twelve issues or would you prefer to test the response by advertising in six issues to begin with?"

The salesman of a service can ask:

"Would you prefer to have the office cleaned early in the morning or late at night?"

A salesman should carry his own order forms or a writing pad. When the prospect states a preference, he must write it down. At that stage, the prospect will either keep silent or say: "Wait a minute. I haven't decided yet."

If he is still indecisive, the salesman must continue to sell. The buyer hasn't said "no".

A test of speciality salesmen found that 74% of them used the alternative close. 64% of consumer-goods salesmen used the alternative close with a slight difference. As each line came up, they said: "Do you find the small or the large size sells best?"

They wrote the answer on the order pad and then asked for the quantity.

The alternative close is most frequently used.

The concession close

Sometimes a salesman can offer a prospect a concession— a special discount, quicker delivery, a tie-in with a promotional scheme, allowances for local advertising, and so on. Many salesmen bring the concession into the sale too soon. It should be offered only after a prospect has been sold on all the benefits. A prospect seldom buys because of a concession. Hold it back as a closing aid:

"Our normal delivery is about eight weeks, sir, but I know you will benefit so much from the equipment when it is installed that I am going to put pressure on the works to make a concession in your case. I will see that you get delivery in three weeks. Is that all right, Mr. Brown?"

"These show-cards are very expensive and we are allowed to leave them only when we get orders in gross lots. Because I am sure you will succeed in selling the line, I will make you a concession. You can have the show-card for a trial order of six dozen."

"I am afraid that we don't as a rule supply fixing brackets. You should get these from your local ironmonger. But as this is the first time we have done business together, I will make a concession and arrange for you to have the brackets free."

"I know that you agree with everything we have said. Finally I can offer you some very special credit terms."

By keeping the concession back, you have a strong closing aid.

The summary close

A jury can sit through a long trial lasting many days or even weeks. A juryman may listen attentively to every item of evidence. But he would scarcely be human if he didn't forget some statement by a witness or a remark by a counsel. So, at the end of a trial, a judge summarises the evidence to help the jury. Before this, defence counsel and prosecuting counsel also sum up. During a sale, the salesman, but not the prospect, is on trial—it is a court case in reverse. No judge sums up the evidence. No defence lawyer, in the person of a competitor denounces the goods. The salesman must remind the prospect of all the benefits he has outlined during the sale. He may use the counting method:

"Mr. Brown, just let me make each point clear again. One, you will increase profits. Two, you will give yourself more leisure time . . ."

The salesman cannot repeat every buying benefit in detail. He must be brief. His summary done, he must assume that the order is his and start writing on his order pad or thank the buyer for his decision.

The fear close

The fear close must be used sparingly. Many buyers react unfavourably to it. It can be effective for salesmen of goods in short supply, or fire-extinguishers, insurance, burglar alarms, other safety devices:

> "You will want me to give you cover right away, Mr. Johnson. After all, if someone dropped a lighted match in a waste-paper basket this afternoon and caused a fire, you would bear the loss. When I have your agreement to this policy, we bear the loss."

> "Mr. Brown, as you know, the new Act could impose heavy fines if office conditions were unsatisfactory. You are too good a businessman to take the risk. I will see that you get delivery quickly."

> "With the season approaching our delivery will extend to about six weeks. This won't be of any use to you. Be on the safe side and place your order right now, or competitors will carry stocks before you."

Estate agents probably use this close more than others. They often have a waiting-list for a house and can honestly say: "I am afraid you must make up your mind quickly as there are two or three other people after it."

Verbal-proof story close

Earlier in the sale you may have named to your prospect other satisfied users of your equipment or service. But always try to save one verbal-proof story for the close. You might conclude like this:

> "When I first called on Mr. Smith, of Smith & White, he was very dubious that our products would sell in his shop.

His shop at Kanton is, as you know, very much like your own. He serves the same kind of people and stocks similar goods. I found it hard to convince him then that he would succeed with our merchandise. But he is a man of decision like you, and he placed a trial order. Now it is one of his best-selling lines—and it can be the same in your shop."

Keep back a good story for the close—one that will swing the prospect in your favour.

The isolation close

One major reason usually prevents a prospect from buying. The salesman must isolate it in order to answer it. He asks the prospect for any such reasons and writes them down.

"Let me be perfectly clear about what you want, Mr. Brown," he should say, and then begin to write: One, you don't like the standard finish. Two you cannot wait three months for delivery. Three, you want three months' credit from the date of installation. Is that so, Mr. Brown?"

Mr. Brown agrees, and then the salesman takes each point and shows how it can be overcome. At last he isolates the main reason that the prospect does not sign the order. This may be lack of three months' credit terms.

"All that separates us then, Mr. Brown, is that you need extended credit facilities. Let me telephone our accounts department now, and I will get it settled right away."

Influencing-the-mind close

Salesmen of certain products cannot close an order. For instance, ethical pharmaceuticals are advertised only in medical journals and can be sold only through prescription. The doctor doesn't buy them, and the chemist does so only when he gets a prescription for the drug. Although the salesman cannot close the order, he must so influence the mind of the doctor that he will prescribe his drugs. He again obtains "yes" responses, and may say at the end of the sales presentation: "You will probably think it a good idea if I call on Smith's the chemists and tell them to be sure and have a stock available."

Or: "You will find this drug so helpful that I am sure you will prescribe it over and over again, so I had better call at the chemist and advise him."

The sale cannot be closed, but the doctor's mind can be influenced; that, after all, is the same as a close.

Closing on a minor point

The salesman deciding to close on a minor point assumes that the order is his, that all major objections have been overcome. He will then use some trial closes:

"Our goods are very carefully packed, but if any should arrive damaged, let us know right away and you will get immediate replacements. How many will you have, then, Mr. Brown?"

"I will have three sets of drawings for the installation sent to you tomorrow so that your engineers can get down to studying them. Then they will be ready to fix the equipment in three months' time. Is that all right, Mr. Jones?"

"You mention, Mr. Smith, that you are a pretty good handyman yourself. You could probably fix this yourself then, without calling in a contractor. I will just write down details."

When you close on a minor point, you lose nothing. If the prospect does not give a definite reply, you continue to sell.

CLOSE THAT ORDER

You can use these closing techniques in any combination. You can use the summary close with the alternative close. Or you can use all the closes at one time, though it is never necessary. But make no mistakes as you near the close. Fear stops a prospect buying. He is afraid he may lose money, afraid he is buying the wrong stock, afraid of what his managing director might say. You must calm his fears and reassure him. You must close the sale in a positive manner. There must be no negative thinking.

Until a sale is closed, you are just a conversationalist. The closing of the sale makes you a salesman.

CHAPTER XIV

OBJECTIONS—AND HOW TO OVERCOME THEM

"Welcome objections," said the lecturer. "They show that the prospect is interested in your proposition." The audience nodded agreement, and instinctively I shook my head the opposite way. For many years we were told that sales objections were good for us, that they helped the sale along by involving the prospect in it. I think this is pure fantasy. There is no virtue in answering each objection competently when, with more forethought, it could have been forestalled before it was brought to light.

Whether sales executives welcome objections or dispute their value, all will agree that a salesman should never argue with the prospect or customer. But when he raises a strong objection, an argument must follow. The salesman must prove that the objection is invalid. For this, he must also prove that the prospect is wrong, that he has not thought clearly, or that he is so dim-witted that he cannot follow logical reasoning. If that is not tantamount to an argument, what is?

Many ways of answering objections are designed to smooth the ruffled feelings of the prospect, but no one should want to be a ruffle-smoother.

For many years I was on the 'welcome the objections' bandwaggon. But I am a little wiser today than I was yesterday.

Now I believe that a salesman should answer objections before they are raised. It is never easy to turn a "no" into a "yes", so why risk a "no"? For example, you may visit an outfitter for a shirt. You ask for one in pale grey. The assistant hasn't one in stock, but shows you a shirt in pale grey with a dark grey stripe. "Do you like this?" he asks. "No", you reply. "I don't think stripes are fashionable any more."

The salesman quickly says: "Well, we sell a lot of them."

"Possibly you do," you answer, rather coldly, "but I don't think they are fashionable."

The assistant can argue; he won't win. He has inferred that you are not fashion-conscious, that you are not aware that striped shirts are again being worn. The more he argues, the more loyal you will be to the anti-stripe brigade. You may even like stripes, but you won't admit it to that assistant. For you, it is now a plain shirt—or nothing.

Most of us would respond similarly to the assistant's clumsy answer to the objection: "I don't like striped shirts."

But the scene could be played differently. The assistant doesn't have a plain grey shirt in stock, but the nearest to it is a plain grey with a stripe. He guesses that you may object to the pattern. So he forestalls you by saying: "As you know, sir, stripes have come right back into fashion again. Here is the very latest in grey, with a darker grey stripe. I thought that you would like to see it. It does something for the shirt, don't you think, sir?"

"Sir" will probably buy.

Objections must never be avoided or evaded. Once raised they must be answered, but the professional salesman can *sell* them away. He *sells* them away by listing every objection that could be raised against his products or service, and then by working out answers. He adapts these as part of his sales sequence to stop the objections being raised.

Here are some instances:

1. A salesman is demonstrating a car. He knows that it is rather sluggish when pulling away from a standing start. So he says: "We have purposely avoided a jerky or racy getaway from a standing start. Most people know the dangers of trying to get ahead of other motorists when the

traffic lights change to green. But the main reason that this car is made to glide away instead of jumping off is to save petrol. It helps you to get at least twenty-eight miles to the gallon. That appeals to you, Mr. Brown, doesn't it?"

The objection, "Why doesn't the car get away faster?" has been forestalled.

2. A salesman of a fire-extinguisher knows that it is a large object and that prospects may complain of its size. He says: "Mr. Jones, one of the advantages of our extinguisher is its size. Because it is fairly large and robustly built, it holds 50% more water than the average extinguisher—just the extra you may need to kill a fire completely. And it can be easily seen, sir—everyone knows where it is. So many smaller types are put away in a drawer, and no one can find one when it is wanted. You like this design, don't you, Mr. Brown?"

The objection, "It seems too large for a private house" has been forestalled.

3. A salesman knows that he cannot deliver his products quickly. He says: "I know, Mr. White, that you will want us to rush delivery, but I also know that nothing would get past you if it were not manufactured to the highest standards. Our quality products have to pass through six different tests. Mr. White, some buyers never plan ahead. They buy from hand to mouth, and then complain that deliveries are late or that the quality of the goods is not up to standard. It is good to know that you are not like that, and that is why we can be of such good service to you. You will have perfectly finished goods delivered in nine weeks."

The objection, "I can get them quicker elsewhere," has been forestalled.

Some objections cannot be treated in this way. The more

trifling ones can, indeed, be welcomed. A woman might say: "I wonder if this hat really suits me?" This is not an objection. She wants confirmation that it suits her.

However skilfully a salesman builds his presentation, he cannot reduce his objections by more than 50%; the rest must be answered efficiently and effectively.

Don't pounce

Our sales training courses include sessions devoted to the answering of objections. Salesmen tell us of difficult objections they must overcome. We have not heard a new one for many, many years. They all fall into similar patterns.

A prospect might raise this objection: "Your casing is made of stainless steel, but I can get something very similar in Tifelin which, I believe, will give far better service."

The salesman meeting this specific objection regularly believes it is peculiar to his own trade. Its only peculiarity is in the technicalities or the words. Customers of all kinds claim that a competitor gives better delivery, more durable containers, or better display material. The salesman must stress the many benefits of his product or service until they exceed the benefits of the competitors' products.

Salesmen soon find the best answers to particular objections. Even the novice will, after a few weeks on the road, know every objection that can be raised and will have good answers for them.

Both experienced salesmen and new recruits are inclined to give pat answers to every buyer's query. Just as the pouncer will never let anyone finish a story but will always interrupt to cap it or to end it, so too many salesmen pounce when objections are raised. They know what the prospect is about to ask as soon as he begins to speak.

This is typical of a pouncer at work.

"Yes," says the prospect, "that's all very well, but the lining . . ."

In jumps the pouncer: "You need not worry about the lining. We can strengthen it by using an interlining as well."

The prospect has not been allowed to finish. His objection has been swept aside as if it were of no consequence. He may not even be happy with an interlining. He may prefer a lining of a different material altogether.

The first rule then, is to allow the prospect to state his objection in full. He must not be interrupted and, even more important, the salesman must *look* as though he is interested in what he is being told. He must not suggest that he has heard it all before and is impatient to give a quick answer.

No one likes a 'Smart Alec'. When a salesman pounces, he appears too clever. When he doesn't concentrate on what the prospect is saying, he loses his confidence. Attend to the prospect's objection, and he will listen to your answer.

When?

Should an objection be handled in the same way as a request for a price? This is often asked. It may be correct to hold back the price until benefits are built up, but delay cannot help an objection. The prospect knows that he must be given a price eventually, but, if an objection is avoided, he may believe it to be unanswerable. It, therefore, looms very large in his mind, and benefits may not always reduce this mountain to a molehill. All objections must be answered as soon as they are made. They must be so satisfactorily cleared that the prospect's full attention can be given to the sales sequence.

Observe

Look at the prospect's face. When you discuss a problem with your wife, or a friend, you will soon know whether you have won the argument. Whenever you have said: "You don't look very happy about it," you have sensed the uncertainty expressed in a face. If a prospect shows concern, you must assume that you have not cleared up the objection for him.

Repeat the objection

A salesman may find himself answering an objection which the prospect has not actually raised.

When an objection is voiced, be sure you fully understand it. The prospect wants to know that you are giving it deep consideration. So repeat the objection to the prospect. If possible adapt it slightly so that it sounds more favourable to you. As an instance:

"I don't think", says the prospect, "that they will sell here. Our customers are mostly working people and they don't go for this fancy stuff. If they want to spend more money, they usually go to one of the stores."

The salesman replies: "As I see it, Mr. Brown, your customers are mainly working people, who now earn good incomes and may not come to you for this very high-quality product . . ."

Then the objection is answered.

The apparent-agreement technique

We know the relaxed prospect is ready to buy. We know that a relaxed salesman can sell in a conversational manner, putting the prospect at ease. But even the most relaxed salesman will not prevent a buyer from getting tense at some time or other. He may do so as he is on the point of signing the the order, or just before he raises an objection.

He makes his point, and prepares for the skirmish that he believes will follow.

But no salesman wants to fight. So he must remove the tension from the objection with the apparent agreement technique. He indicates that he is inclined to agree with the objection, and the prospect, thinking he has won his point, relaxes.

The apparent agreement technique is based on the words, "I agree, but." It would operate in its simplest form like this:

"You don't deliver on time."

"I agree, but . . ."

Few salesmen would be quite so abrupt as that, but adapt their replies in such ways as:

"I quite understand why you feel that the colour scheme is wrong, but . . ."

"Yes, you are quite right, Mr. Jones, in thinking at this stage that your shop may not be in the right position for this machine, but . . ."

"There is a lot of truth, Mr. Smith, in your assumption that extra labour might be needed, but . . ."

"I admire you, Mr. Jones, for admitting that the quality may be a little too high for your store, but . . ."

"On the face of it, you are quite correct in believing that it might create an odour, but . . ."

The boomerang technique

The boomerang technique should be reserved to the strong salesman or the representative with utter confidence in his ability to give a 'turnabout' answer. If used without conviction it could antagonise the prospect, for the salesman uses his objection as a sales point.

This is how he does it:

"I can't see any point," says the prospect, "in giving you an order. I am very satisfied with Perks & Co., who have supplied me for more than twenty years."

"Mr. Jones," answers the salesman, "surely that is the very reason why you should open an account with us. Over a twenty-year period there are changes of personnel, and there can be more over the next ten years. By buying from us, you will safeguard your supplies in the future. Now, Mr. Jones, you are a very forward-looking man . . ."

Here is another example:

"I can buy more cheaply," says the prospect, "so I can sell more cheaply and sell more. I'm sorry—I can't buy from you."

"But, Mr. Brown," answers the salesman, "that is the

very reason why you should buy from me. You will make the same profit from selling half as many of our better-quality products as the cheaper ones. You will have more time to serve other customers . . ."

The prospect throws the objection boomerang, and it is sent back to him as a sales point.

Praise the prospect

No prospect likes to be proved wrong and his objections must be handled delicately. If his objection is treated as a discussion point, an argument can be avoided. The prospect should be praised for raising the objection. For example:

"I am very glad you raised that point, Mr. Brown. It shows how seriously you are considering the proposition . . ."

"I am so glad you brought that point forward, Mr. Smith. Obviously the fault is entirely mine for not clarifying the position about consumption of electricity . . ."

You also praise the prospect for remarks made earlier in the sale:

"You will remember, Mr. Brown, that you said just now you thought there would be a recession before the next election. You are probably right, but I can assure you that your turnover will increase whatever the political outlook, if we can carry out the improvements right now . . ."

Make the prospect feel important and he will not believe the objection is so important.

Price objections

Imagine the presence during every sale of an invisible pair of scales. On one scale is the price of a salesman's product or service; on the other scale are the benefits he offers. When a price is mentioned the scale is loaded against the salesman. It is as if a bag holding £100 worth of cash were placed on that scale.

On the other scale, the salesman starts to heap his benefits. He explains how his product's quality gives it long life, increases the buyer's business, satisfies his pride or his sense of caution. As each benefit is placed on the pan, so the scale tilts in favour of the salesman.

The scales are even when the buyer, unable to make up his mind, tries to delay a decision by raising objections. The salesman continues to pile up benefits until, at last, his scale is heavier than the one holding the £100. Then the salesman completes his order.

The price objection can only be beaten when benefits outweigh it. A prospect may not place an order because he thinks he can get a similar product elsewhere at less cost. The salesman keeps stressing the benefits of his service, and also pays special attention to the difference between the price of his product and that of his competitor. For example, a fork-lift truck may cost £1,200. A competitor may have a similar one for £1,120. The salesman should say:

> "You will want to appreciate the position, Mr. Brown, before you decide. You know that you want a fork-lift truck. You know how much it will benefit your business, but you are uncertain which model to buy. Let us consider £80, which is the difference between the price of my truck and the other one you are considering. This is what you will get for your extra £80 . . ."

He then lists all the additional benefits of his truck above those of competitive makes.

When selling against a competitor, therefore, always bring the price down to differences. Let the buyer focus upon a figure far smaller than the total expenditure.

What does it cost

H. Mather, chief training consultant in our sales training division, teaches salesmen to overcome the price objection this way:

> "In almost every sales situation, the price must be justified. This is, of course, always true when it is overtly raised. 'It's too expensive' is a typical comment, and it

can't pass unchallenged. Every sale is an investigation, and it is vital to pinpoint the reasons underlying a buyer's opinion. For example, it is always reasonable to query the word 'expensive'. What does it mean? Expense is not an absolute, and makes sense only in relation to another figure.

Here is an example:

'Mr. Buyer, you say it's too expensive, and you would appear to be right. I agree with you that it costs more than other products, but, when you say expensive, please tell me—in comparison with what?'

"This question begins the process of investigation, and his answer indicates the buyer's reasoning. The answer may be anticipated, for choices are limited.

"If your product/service is not being used, these are the choices:

To use a similar product.
To have a similar service.
To use a similar method.
To use similar raw materials.
To do without altogether.

"The answer gives a basis for discussion. Through product knowledge, an awareness of the customer's needs and of the performance of competitive products, an objective comparison can be made. The process of cost justification can begin.

"Price is an important factor in a sales negotiation, but it does not always dominate the situation. People do not buy on price alone. Sometimes the salesman is more conscious of price than the buyer! The mere use of the word, contributes to the problem. It is an outgoing word, suggesting spending. Salesmen should cultivate the use of the word, 'cost'. This is a commercial word that sounds more professional and suggests investment rather than spending.

"In discussion, and particularly in answer to the question 'How much is it?' salesmen should use 'It costs only . . .' This clearly and simply indicates the salesman's confidence in the offer he is making.

"The price objection, like any other, must be answered in terms of benefits. The cost of the product/service, irrespective of the amount, must be shown as a valuable investment for the purchaser. The analysis of value is cost-justification. Value has three distinct and important elements, and each must be explained and illustrated to the buyer in terms of benefits.

EFFICIENCY

"Every product or service has a demonstrable and measurable rating of performance. This is its efficiency.

ECONOMY

"Every buyer looks for economy, and the features of a product or service that provide it must be fully described. Economies, not technicalities, are the reasons for buying.

"Faster production, savings of time and labour, more miles per gallon, longer life in use—these are a few examples.

PROFIT

"To the buyer concerned with the distribution and resale of a product—a wholesaler or a retailer—one important aspect of value is profit. The product must be efficient and economical in performance, but it must be shown to be profitable. All buyers do not immediately grasp the true situation. A first glance at the proposed percentage mark-up may suggest that the product will be less profitable than existing stock items, or others on offer. There may be instances of this, but it is important to investigate and establish the true facts. For example, product 'A' is bought at 9 units and sells at 12 units, but product 'B' costs 8 and sells at 12. The obvious reaction is that product 'B' is more profitable. But profit on one item of sale is not the only consideration. Other factors must be rated:

What will be the repeat-business level?
Is the quality right?
Is the pack attractive?

"Most important, what advertising, merchandising or other promotional activity is part of the offer? This support for the distributor sales effort is valuable. All aspects of this must be stressed to a buyer as an aid to his decision.

SERVICE

"A constant factor of any offer is service. The support of the distributor is a specialised form of service, but it exists in many other forms.

"The advice of a technical representative is service.

"The activity of the manufacturers' design staff on behalf of a potential customer is service.

"The training of the customer's staff in the correct operation of newly-installed equipment is service.

"Not only are they service but they are benefits, and should be sold as part of the value of the offer.

"Each element of value must be fully explained, and the buyer must understand how it will benefit him. Not only must he understand, but he must accept that the additional cost is justified in terms of value."

Delay excuses

Even efficient buyers who place orders every day do not always come to quick decisions. Regular buyers in works, offices and shops can be equally slow. Shopkeepers place orders for consumer goods and would not delay signing an order for their routine requirements. If, however, they are asked to buy new products, or capital equipment for their shops, they often postpone a decision.

Many of us are undecided when we are in a position to buy. Even buying a hat, we often cannot make up our mind. When negotiating for a house, it is difficult to decide whether A or B is better. We are all tarred with the same brush, and we all invent delay excuses. If we look at an item of furniture in a shop, we may tell the assistant that we want to check our own furnishings before a decision. When an insurance salesman calls, we try to put him off until we have more time, perhaps after our holiday. This is, of course, sheer nonsense. If it is right to take out additional insurance, then the quicker the better. Nothing is gained by delaying matters for a few weeks. If we are presented with a detailed proposition by a salesman, we should be able to make our mind up on the spot. There is nothing new to be learned at a later interview. But we will still try to delay matters.

When a delay excuse is used, a prospect is only partly sold. His interest has been aroused, but not his enthusiasm. If he suggests you should call back at a later date, he will think of all the reasons *not to buy* before you come again. He will not think of a single reason for placing an order. He may also buy from a competitor before you return.

The salesman must counter these excuses by trying to find the real reason for the delay:

"I appreciate, Mr. Brown, that you would like to leave matters for two or three weeks, but what is there to think over? Perhaps I haven't explained everything clearly to you. Again, let me go through all the reasons that this product can be of service to you, and perhaps you will tell me if there is any point you are not clear about."

"I can understand that you want to consult your partner, but is that fair to him? He won't have the complete proposition before him as I have tried to put it to you. So he may veto the whole idea, and this could cause a loss to both of you."

"Mr. Jackson, I do understand that you would like to see me again in about three weeks. Before I started this job, I had six months of intensive training and I have now been with the company for five years. All this has helped me to give a better service to our customers. It also means that I have been trained to explain to you fully every facet of our service. If you wish to put our proposition to your Board of Directors, you will agree, Mr. Jackson, that it would be almost impossible to be fair to everyone. No doubt, you would prefer me to address your Board. But don't you think they would prefer you to come to a decision that will benefit the whole business?"

"Mr. Smith, you are in business to make profits. Isn't that right? Now when this equipment is installed, you will make extra profits right away. Let's take a small amount of £200 profit in six months. (This may be from extra turnover, reduced absenteeism or labour costs, etc.) This would mean that our equipment, which now costs £1,000 will cost you £1,200 in six months, because we must then include the £200 you have lost. You are a man of decision, Mr. Smith, don't you think it is right for you to decide now?"

"Mr. Brown, you have built up your business by making decisions—decisions based on facts. I have given you all the facts, and so I know that you will, like Mr. Whiting of Smith and Company, place your order right away. As I told you, he has been delighted with his purchase and so will you be."

No call for goods

This objection is raised by retailers. The prospect takes it into his head that there is no call for certain merchandise, or that he has no room for a new line as the standard ones sell well.

A similar objection is: "I don't want to open any more accounts."

These are not true objections. What the prospect means is:

"I don't believe there will be any demand for *your* goods."

"I don't believe that I need *your* new line."

"I don't think that it would benefit me to open an account with *you*."

No retailer would stay in business if he did not add new lines to his stock and if he didn't open new accounts from time to time. He doesn't want to do business with *you* because he believes that he cannot sell *your* merchandise. But his belief is mere guesswork. How can he know that a certain line will not sell if he doesn't stock it? He may explain that his decision is based on experience with similar lines, but the operative word is 'similar'. These goods were not exactly the same as yours, and, even if they were, a good salesman should take an order.

A high-grade jam that does not sell in a shop one year may sell 12 or 15 months later. A district is always changing. Some people move out, others move in. Newcomers may prefer a quality jam, buy it, tell their friends, and soon build a business for the retailer. The salesman could say this, if his line were entirely new:

"Mr. Jones, I appreciate the way you think, but may I ask you a question? You are a gentleman's outfitter. Do you think you could sell hamburgers?"

The prospect will ridicule the idea.

"But, Mr. Jones, if you fixed a notice outside your shop with the words, 'Wimpy Bar for Hamburgers!', I guarantee that someone would walk in and ask for a hamburger. It is the same with this new line of ties. They are higher-priced than your standard lines but if you display them there will be a demand for them. You lose money all the time you don't stock our 'Top Ten' ties."

The hidden objection

Do honest people always tell the truth? In a play called "Nothing but the Truth," the hero promised to tell the truth for twenty-four hours to win a bet. It led, of course, to endless complications. Such a simple question from a wife as "Do you like my hairstyle?" became almost unanswerable.

Few people tell the truth all day and every day. Those who buy, lie—at almost every sales interview. They lie about prices; they lie about deliveries. And they lie when they raise objections. They are often unwilling to tell the salesman the true objection. When a prospect says: "You are too dear," does he really believe it? When he says, "I want to put matters off to speak to my partner," does he intend just this? When he invites the salesman to send him a leaflet, will he read it as promised or will he throw it into the waste-paper basket?

Prospects make excuses to conceal the true reason for not placing an order. A retailer may be short of money. He may have a good business but be temporarily embarrassed by an overdraft. A salesman from a well-known company calls upon him. The retailer knows that the company has a tough credit policy. If payment is not made within a short time, the accountant will write a strong letter. If there is further delay, dark hints of legal action will be dropped. So the retailer tells the salesman that he won't open an account because he doesn't want any new accounts or he doesn't believe that the line will sell, or he thinks the prices are wrong.

The managing director of a large company may be discussing the installation of capital equipment. But he may be managing director in name only, and own a mere couple of shares in the company. The main shares might be held by a holding company with a rule that no orders for capital equipment be placed without the sanction of the accountant. So

16

the managing director makes excuses to a salesman wanting an on-the-spot decision. He may object to a price or the profitability of a product, and insist upon the matter being put in cold storage. If the salesman had known that the sanction of the company's accountant was required, he would have acted differently.

Another prospect, technically untrained, may have been blinded with the salesman's technical knowledge. He will not admit that he is not qualified to understand all the intricacies of the machine. Instead, he will make excuses to disguise the true reason.

The advertising-space salesman is regularly greeted with: "Yes, I will certainly remember you and put your name on my schedule, but I cannot book any space in your magazine now as we have spent our allocation for the next six months." This is rarely true. No one likes to miss a good opportunity, and few firms cannot take additional space if they want to do so. The real reason for not buying might be that the advertising manager does not believe in the authenticity of the circulation figure given by the salesman.

A high percentage of sales are lost because the salesman has not found the hidden objection. It can easily be found in such a way as this:

"So, Mr. Smith, you don't want to buy at the moment because you believe the unit is too large and the cost of installation would be too high. *And your other reason for not buying is . . .?*"

The last sentence is given with a rising inflection in the voice. The prospect will generally reveal his hidden objection.

As an alternative, the prospect could be asked, after the main objections: ". . . *And, Mr. Jones, what else is bothering you?*" The truth will probably emerge.

The managing director may hesitantly explain that he cannot buy without the sanction of the holding company's accountant. The salesman will then know how to act. The prospect without technical training might say: "Well, you know, I don't know if I am technically qualified to come to a decision." The salesman will then appreciate that he hasn't been talking in the language of the prospect, and he must translate his technicalities into everyday terms.

The representative of the company that insists upon quick settlement of accounts might hear this from the retailer: "Well, the trouble with you people is that you always want payment on the dot." The salesman can then offer extended credit if he is allowed to do so, or can ask what credit the retailer requires so that he can check that it is permissible.

NOT WELCOME

So you must not welcome or encourage objections. You must distinguish between an objection and a buying signal, which are often similar. When a customer says, "I can buy cheaper," it is an objection. When he says, "Is that the best price you can offer?" he is giving a buying signal. Study the techniques of answering objections in the knowledge that the professional salesman will try to forestall them.

CHAPTER XV

HOW TO SUCCEED QUICKLY

Here are four short case-histories. The first concerns a salesman of consumer goods to grocers. He became sales manager. The second was a salesman of sewing machines to housewives, mainly from leads from his company's chain of shops. He became Southern sales manager. The third was a salesman of paint-spraying equipment to factories. He became, first, Northern sales manager, and then sales manager for Ireland. And the fourth man, a salesman of motor accessories in the Midlands, became sales director.

Hundreds of men have achieved similar success within a short time, about a year, by putting a single lesson into practice.

The common factor

Salesmen come to our offices every day for advice, and the interview follows a pattern. The salesman is greeted, asked to sit down and tell us his troubles. He begins diffidently: "Well, Mr. Tack, it is all a little difficult because you know the company employing me. I would like to emphasise therefore, that all the time I have been with them I have been very loyal, and I am still loyal . . ."

There is a pause after "loyal", and it is invariably followed with "but". "But", says the man, "I feel so frustrated with them. That is why I have called to see you."

These salesmen give different reasons for their frustration. The middle-aged representative is often frustrated because a younger man has received the promotion he coveted for himself. A salesman in a large organisation is often frustrated because he gets too many instruction memoranda and too few friendly letters.

And so they come in a constant stream—men frustrated because their sales manager doesn't understand them, because they are not earning enough money or not achieving rapid promotion. Lack of promotion is at the root of most frustration. They want to succeed but believe their efforts are ignored. When we ask the salesman about his sales figures and how they compare with others in the organisation, he usually admits ruefully that he has not achieved spectacular results.

One of these reasons is given:

> "They don't advertise enough."
> "The service department lets me down."
> "Deliveries are bad."
> "Sales promotion material is poor."
> "They won't let me have a car."
> "I have a territory which has been worked to death."
> "Prices are not competitive."
> "The designs are out of date."
> "I don't get good backing."

If these frustrations and excuses were limited to a few salesmen in a specialised field, there might be some substance in them. As men in every sphere of selling, men of all ages and experience have the same excuses, the conclusion must be that they are wrong and their companies right.

Frustration from failure to increase sales is caused by some weakness in the salesman. All salesmen cannot be outstanding. But each one has the power to increase his sales, however good or bad his selling aptitude may be.

This book has been written to teach men to train themselves into top-ranking salesmen, and some readers will profit by it. Less skilled men can increase sales by learning the lesson in this chapter. Sales can increase by 20%, 30%, or even 40%. The £500-a-month man can achieve a turnover of £650 a month. The better representative with a monthly turnover of £1,000 can increase his sales to £1,300 a month or more. It can happen—and it has happened time and time again.

You must aim for the top by applying every lesson in this book. But salesmanship alone is not enough. It must be combined with an *extra*, and that is our subject now. This extra can make an ordinary salesman very good, a first-class salesman outstanding. Outstanding salesmen achieve promotion. *The men whose case-histories we summarised at the start of this chapter succeeded because they each increased sales about 30%.*

Can you do it?

Thousands of salesmen will read this book. Will they all become outstanding? Will they all increase their sales by 30% or 40%? If more than 10,000 salesmen could increase their sales by 30%, business would be revolutionised. It is theoretically possible, but in practice does not work. For any group of men and women contains the below-average, the average, and the above-average.

Take fifty housewives who consider themselves practical, efficient, and hardworking. Within that group there would be inefficient housewives. A woman who has been cooking for twenty years is not necessarily a good cook. Experience is not always enough. There must also be the ability to learn from experience and the willingness to apply the lesson learned.

This also applies to a group of managing directors. Some of them are very inefficient, and muddle through. The turnover of large organisations can fall sharply in a year through inefficiencies at the top. A group of managing directors would contain men of all abilities, from the outstanding to the mediocre. The same would be found amongst groups of doctors, farmers, builders, or dentists. And amongst salesmen.

What do most average or below-average men have in common? Vast research would be needed to find out. From my own experience, however, I have found a common denominator for men doomed to be below average in their jobs. It may not be their own fault, but could be blamed on heredity, upbringing, environment, glands, or the size of the brain. Whatever the reason, they will resist any plan or policy that conflicts with their preconceived ideas.

If they are doctors or dentists, their minds will be closed to new advances in medicine or dental surgery. Some time ago a new high-speed drill was introduced for dentists. The go-ahead ones soon made use of it. At a conference I met many dentists (I wasn't attending it—just staying at the same hotel) and discussed with them the benefits I had found since my dentist used the new drill. But many objected. Many minds were closed. One dentist thought there would be a lack of control with the drill; another believed it to be highly dangerous. That was a few years ago. Many of them may now have the drill, but others will still be using the outdated implements.

Top men, who have achieved a high position through their own abilities and not because they were booked for it through birth, will always listen to new ideas. They are usually eager to try something different, something new. It is impossible to convince men without this breadth of vision that a change is necessary.

The below-average salesman has exactly the same faults as the below-average managing director. He closes his mind to any idea he believes is beyond his ability. If he is afraid to use the telephone, he insists that there is no advantage in telephoning for appointments. If he is scared of opening new accounts, he will kid himself that he is so fully occupied with servicing customers that he has no time to call on anyone else.

The man with the closed mind bases his decisions upon newspaper headlines, which he repeats as his own views. If he has a Y car, it is the best of all cars. If he has holidayed for fifteen years running in Ilfracombe, then there is no better place; he will find arguments against foreign holidays claiming that they are too expensive and breed all kinds of illnesses.

A salesman can easily judge whether he is below average by his reaction to tuition. He may say, after he has read this book: "Mr. Tack's companies sell capital equipment, but I sell consumer goods. The book is slanted towards capital-goods selling and most of it doesn't apply to me."

Another may say: "The book seems to be aimed at salesmen of consumer products. I can't use these techniques for top-level negotiations."

The insurance salesman will insist that his type of selling is more arduous than others, but the salesman of ethical pharmaceuticals will tell him that selling insurance is child's play compared with persuading doctors to prescribe drugs.

Every lesson in this book has been tried and tested over many years, not only in Britain but throughout the world. There can be no doubt that every lesson is applicable to every kind of selling.

Look back over the various chapters. You must agree that, whatever a man is selling, he must have good health. Relaxing leads to good health.

You will agree that ease of manner helps a salesman, and this is acquired through conversational selling.

Every representative knows that a fundamental factor in his job is that he must sell himself. This is now known as human relations. A knowledge of human relations influences the personality of a salesman. You cannot disagree with that, can you?

Whether he is selling timber or ties, the salesman who is disliked will find it much harder to be a success. All salesmen live by the words they use; therefore, if you evolve better sentences, selling techniques must improve.

But, despite all this, most readers of this book will still say: "This doesn't apply to me." But a minority will say: "I will *make* this apply to me." These are the salesmen who can achieve dramatic results within twelve months.

Of course, it would be absurd for anyone to claim that most salesmen could increase their sales by 30%. I claim only that some salesmen, the minority, will do so. They are now above the average or are determined to make themselves above average.

These readers will make this effort—and I hope you will be amongst them. Then irrespective of whether you sell consumer goods or capital equipment, advertising or products for export, whether you have been with your company for one year or ten, you can, during the next twelve months, increase your turnover by up to 40%.

The time factor

We once researched into the working habits of nearly 1,000 salesmen of every type of product and service. Questionnaires were completed, a number of men interviewed, and others collaborated with a sales consultant. The result not only astounded the salesmen, but astonished us. It showed that nearly every salesman wasted between 30% and 40% of his selling time every day.

So any salesman, whatever his ability, can increase his sales by about 40% a year. Most of those who co-operated in the survey were average men, working with average success. Although the result disturbed most of them, they did not change their ways.

The salesman, determined to succeed quickly, can learn an important lesson from this survey. He must find the missing 40% of his working time and use it to increase his sales by the same percentage. With more time, a salesman can open more accounts, make more cold-canvass calls, help with merchandising, use the telephone more effectively to make appointments, interview more people.

If eight daily calls are made instead of six, sales must go up. But most men will say that six calls are their maximum

17

and eight an impossibility. By better use of time, the impossible becomes possible. Here are some of the conclusions of our survey.

The early morning call

If a customer or prospective customer is available at an early hour of the morning and a salesman makes his first call one hour later, he loses an hour a day. Many builders, garage proprietors, newsagents and farmers start work early in the morning—and they can be visited from 8 a.m. onwards.

If a salesman understands human relations, he can win over the prospect who appears to object to an early call from him. We found that more than 80% of top executives arrived before their staff in the morning. Men who sell capital goods equipment to top management do not realise that they can gain interviews so early.

Early calls will get you some interviews. Naturally, if a business does not open its doors before nine o'clock, it is useless to call earlier.

The time a salesman leaves his home in the morning, is irrelevant. The important thing is the time of the first call. He is not working when he is travelling. A salesman may have to leave his house at 6.30 a.m. or 7 a.m. for an early call at 8.30 a.m.

One hour a day saved tots up to five hours a week. This is twenty hours a month, or 240 hours a year. An hour wasted every day equals the loss of thirty working days a year. Think about that.

The coffee break

Most salesmen taking part in the survey had a coffee break in the morning. This lasted about fifteen minutes—or the equivalent of about seven days a year. Can any salesman afford to throw away one week every year?

Evening work

Salesmen waste one hour every evening, and two hours every Friday evening. They explain that no one will see them after five o'clock, but if a prospective customer is open for trading until six o'clock, then a call can be made up to that time. No salesman would enjoy it. With offices closing and commuters going home, he wants to follow suit.

But the man determined to succeed will make the extra call. One more call each evening gives hundreds of extra interviews each year; even one more in a week will add up to fifty extra calls in a year.

Planning

Most salesmen plan their work well, but they should constantly check that time is not wasted through bad planning.

Saturday morning work

Every salesman cannot work on Saturday mornings, but many can.

In our industrial divisions, with men selling to factories, shops, offices, retailers, and consultants, every man works on Saturday mornings. Orders can be obtained on a Saturday. Few believe it, but it is true.

Meeting friends

Newcomers to selling soon make friends with other representatives. Salesmen who have worked on the road for many years have a host of friends. They meet them day after day, and they stop work for a chat. They gossip outside shops, offices, factories, and farms. Our survey showed that ten days a year are lost by men who talk to friends met casually.

Making purchases

If a man worked in an office, he would not leave his desk to make a household purchase. But salesmen believe they are in a different category from office workers. They give themselves privileges not allowed to indoor men. But they haven't special privileges, only added responsibilities. Most salesmen will make private purchases during the day, and waste time better spent in selling.

Taking children to school

No office worker would tell his manager that he cannot get to the office before 10 a.m. because he must take his children to school. Many salesmen, because they have cars—often company cars—start work late because they consider it a duty to take their children to school in the morning. This may help a wife, but it undermines family security in the long run. Most wives put security first.

The telephone

Many hours can be wasted by the wrong use of a telephone.

A salesman telephoning his office will rarely state his business, get a reply, and put the receiver down. He will have a lengthy chat with the receptionist. He will give his sales manager a dossier of the illnesses throughout the family and a full weather report.

Telephone conversations must be cut short.

Calling at the office

Many salesmen will find any excuses to visit head office or a branch office. They tell themselves that important matters must be discussed, that they must collect leaflets, that they must explain a quotation in detail.

Most of these reasons are invalid. Unless a salesman is summoned to it, he should keep well away from the office. These visits waste time.

Family favours

No man working in a shop would ask for time off to meet a relative off a train or to attend a children's party. But salesmen get home early to attend a children's party. They will leave late in the morning because someone must be met at a station. This is wrong, very wrong. It is a form of cheating.

Car breakdowns

When a salesman's car breaks down, he often uses it as an excuse to stop work for that day. He rarely thinks of alternative transport to reach customers and prospects; he lingers near the garage until the work is done.

Talking too much

One of the biggest time-wasters derives from a salesman's inability to listen more and talk less. No prospect is absorbed by a salesman's home life or his views. No salesman should bore a customer with weather reports, the beauty of the roses he grows in his garden, the accident he saw on the M.1, how his children are getting on at school, or how much he enjoyed his holiday.

If a prospect wants to tell the salesman about his holiday, he must listen for the prospect warms towards a listener. If the prospect, out of politeness, concludes with: "Did you enjoy your holiday?" the answer must be brief "Yes, thank you." The salesman then sells benefits. Five or ten minutes can be saved at every call by listening more and talking less.

THERE ARE MORE

Many more time-wasters could be listed. But you will, or will not, want to pay the price of success. If you do not accept that you waste time, then keep a diary for the next four weeks. Write down how you spend every minute of your selling day. You will soon see that time has been wasted. Make use of this missing time, which could be as much as 40% of the whole, and your sales will increase.

I mentioned men who tell me that they are frustrated. One point should be clarified. If any man is completely happy with the work he is doing, and with his income—and his wife is also satisfied—then there is no need for extra effort. If a wife never suggests that she would like to move to a better house, or stop sharing with her in-laws, that she wants a holiday abroad or extra clothes, then the husband is lucky.

Such men can go on their way happily and enjoy every day of their life. But how many are like this? Most men that I meet are frustrated because they want promotion, they want to feel more important. The wives are frustrated too, because of their husbands' lack of success. For these men, surely the price is worth paying?

There has been much talk for many years about improving the status of the salesman. You are the master of your own fate, and you can train yourself to succeed in selling and to reap its rewards.

INDEX